THE
HIGH-PROTEIN
HEARTY DISHES THAT EVEN CARNIVORES WILL LOVE
VEGETARIAN
COOKBOOK

Katie Parker

Recipe Developer and Photographer

Kristen Smith

Ph.D, R.D., L.D.

THE
HIGH-PROTEIN

HEARTY DISHES THAT EVEN CARNIVORES WILL LOVE

VEGETARIAN
COOKBOOK

Katie Parker

Recipe Developer and Photographer

Kristen Smith

Ph.D, R.D., L.D.

The Countryman Press

A division of W.W. Norton & Company

Independent Publishers Since 1923

The Countryman Press
www.countrymanpress.com

A division of W. W. Norton & Company, Inc.
500 Fifth Avenue, New York, NY 10110
www.wwnorton.com

978-1-58157-263-6

10 9 8 7 6 5

For my mom, who is simply the best.
Without you I wouldn't be here . . .
both literally and figuratively.

THE
HIGH-PROTEIN

HEARTY DISHES THAT EVEN CARNIVORES WILL LOVE

VEGETARIAN
COOKBOOK

KATIE

Anyone who knew me for the first 18 years of my life is likely (and understandably) confused by the fact that I've written a cookbook. Throughout high school I ate the exact same lunch every day: a bagel with light cream cheese, baked chips, and applesauce. My food was beige and my nutrients were low, but I was young and active and didn't think twice about it. At the time I assumed the light cream cheese and baked chips made my lunch healthy. It all made perfect, simple sense.

I was fortunate to attend a college with an incredibly diverse cafeteria. Initially I leaned into my comfortable foods: peanut butter toast, cheese pizza, and of course bagels with cream cheese. After a few months (and a few extra pounds, if we're being honest), I started branching out. I quickly realized I felt much better when I ate more protein and fewer processed foods. My eating evolved throughout my four years of college, and when I graduated and began cooking for myself, I found that eating healthy foods not only made me feel better, but being in the kitchen relieved my "holy crap I just entered the real world" stress like nothing else.

In the meantime, I began dating Ryan, who happens to be a big-time hunter and carnivore. Having him in my life (and in my kitchen) added a little extra challenge to my cooking, because I wanted to create hearty, meat-free meals that both of us could enjoy. He came up with the blog name "Veggie and the Beast," and I've been sharing my recipes online ever since.

When people learn I'm a vegetarian, the first question that follows is always about protein. Meat is known for its protein, so it makes sense that people would wonder what non-meat-eaters do to fulfill their protein quota. This book is my long-winded

answer to that question. When I started writing this book, I planned to use protein powder in some of the recipes. However, as I started researching and testing protein powders, it was difficult to find one that both tasted good in recipes and was free of artificial sweeteners. When I tried to develop recipes with unflavored protein powder, I found that they just weren't as delicious as their whole food counterparts. For this reason, I've opted to use protein-dense whole foods to keep things both tasty and high protein. I think it's the best of both worlds.

Each main course in this book has at least 10 grams of protein, and each snack/side/dessert has at least 6 grams. When I realized I could hit those benchmarks without protein powder or supplements, I decided to go for it.

If you're wondering where the protein comes from, here is an overview of the main sources used throughout the book:

- Beans
- Lentils
- Nuts and seeds
- Nut butters
- Whole grains
- Dairy

There are some recipes where I use tofu and tempeh (soy) and seitan ("wheat meat"). When buying tofu and tempeh I always purchase an organic variety because of the prevalence of genetically modified soy. With all of these products, I prefer to buy them unflavored, so that I can add my own seasonings and spices that make them go with each dish.

My goal with this book is to debunk the myth that vegetarian food lacks protein, and to show how easy and accessible vegetarian cooking can be. The recipes in this book truly do reflect the way that I eat every day. I hope these recipes inspire vegetarians and meat-eaters alike to see protein in a new way.

KRISTEN

When Katie asked me to collaborate with her on this vegetarian and high-protein cookbook, I jumped at the opportunity to provide nutritional input and my perspective as a registered dietitian. Although I have gone through periods of my life when I relied more heavily on vegetarian foods, I am not currently a vegetarian. I do, however, make it a point to provide vegetarian and meatless meals to my family several times a week. In working with Katie, I was lucky enough to get firsthand access to 75 incredibly inventive and tasty vegetarian (and sometimes vegan) recipes that my husband and toddler also eat and enjoy!

According to The Vegetarian Resource Group, vegetarians are those who do not eat meat, fish, or poultry, whereas vegans are vegetarians who do not eat or use any animal products (this includes milk, cheese, other dairy, eggs, honey, wool, silk, leather, or other goods). Vegetarian cooking and vegetarian lifestyles appeal to many people for a variety of reasons including health benefits, ecological and religious concerns, personal beliefs, compassion for animals, dislike of the taste and/or texture of meat, and more.

Throughout my career as a registered dietitian, I have counseled vegetarian and vegan clients and worked with them to ensure that they are receiving adequate nutrition from their diets. Since vegetarians do not consume meat, fish, or poultry, people often assume that they are not able to get enough protein in their diets – in fact, this is a common misconception. Fortunately, there are several vegetarian protein sources (many of which are included in this cookbook) that can be prepared in a variety of ways and contribute high-quality protein. The Academy of Nutrition and Dietetics has confirmed that a vegetarian diet can meet all known nutrient needs. By consuming a varied diet that includes adequate calories (providing enough energy to maintain weight) and a mixture of proteins throughout the day, vegetarians are well-positioned to meet their protein and other nutrient requirements.

Protein is an essential nutrient, which means that we cannot survive without it. It provides structure and function to all cells in the body—it is found in muscle, bone, skin, hair, and nearly every other body part or tissue. Protein is of vital importance to our health, but people are often surprised to learn that we don't actually need to consume it in huge amounts. So how much protein do we actually need per day? The Institute of Medicine recommends that we consume at least 0.8 gram of protein for every kilogram that we weigh (or 0.36 gram of protein for every pound that we weigh); in the United States, the recommended dietary allowance (RDA) of protein for women and men (over the age of 19) is 46 grams and 56 grams of protein per day, respectively. Recipes from this cookbook will help you meet your protein needs with each delicious vegetarian meal and snack.

CHAPTER ONE

BREAKFAST

ROASTED RED PEPPER AND BRIE FRITTATA

SERVES 8

Although scrambled eggs are a great go-to savory breakfast, sometimes it's fun to feel fancy by serving your eggs in frittata form. Frittatas are one of those treasured meals that look impressive, yet are surprisingly easy. This recipe starts with protein-rich eggs, milk, and Greek yogurt, which together bake up fluffy in the oven. Roasted red peppers add a little smoky sweetness to the top, while creamy Brie gives the dish a bit of rich decadence.

INGREDIENTS:

2   tablespoons olive oil

1   clove garlic, minced

1   shallot, diced

10 large eggs

½   cup 1% milk

½   cup 2% plain Greek yogurt

¾   teaspoon fine sea salt

½   teaspoon ground black pepper

¼   teaspoon garlic powder

1   teaspoon dried basil

2   roasted red peppers, thinly sliced (about ½ cup)

6   ounces Brie, rind removed, cut into ½-inch chunks

INSTRUCTIONS:

1. Preheat the oven to 400°F.

2. Heat the olive oil in a 12-inch oven-safe skillet over medium-low heat. Cook the garlic for about 30 seconds, until fragrant. Add the shallot and cook until translucent, about 3 minutes.

3. In a separate bowl, whisk together the eggs, milk, yogurt, salt, pepper, garlic powder, and dried basil. If necessary, use a hand mixer to beat the mixture until the yogurt is fully incorporated. Pour into the skillet.

4. Let the eggs cook in the skillet over medium heat for 5 to 6 minutes, until the bottom is set and the edges are starting to slightly firm up. Place the pepper slices and Brie on top of the frittata, then place the skillet in the oven.

5. Cook in the oven for 12 to 14 minutes, until puffy, lightly golden, and no longer jiggly in the center.

6. Let cool for a few minutes before cutting into eight slices.

NUTRITION INFORMATION PER SERVING:
Calories 216, Calories from Fat 141,
Fat (g) 15.7, Saturated Fat (g) 6.4,
Protein (g) 14.5, Carbohydrate (g) 3.7,
Dietary Fiber (g) 0.4, Cholesterol (mg) 255,
Sodium (mg) 489

CHEESY EGG BAKE MUFFINS

SERVES 6

I made these muffins for my best friend's baby shower, and they were a big hit! They're the perfect brunch finger food, but also make a great portable on-the-go breakfast or snack. They're fluffy and full of flavor from the shallot, basil, spiced eggs, and creamy mozzarella. Put together the eggs, and chop the veggies and bread the night before for an impressive dish that's easy to throw together the morning of an event. If you want to just make them for yourself, you can enjoy the leftovers for days by simply reheating in the microwave.

INGREDIENTS:

7   large eggs

½   cup 2% plain Greek yogurt

½   teaspoon fine sea salt

¼   teaspoon ground black pepper

½   teaspoon garlic powder

½   teaspoon onion powder

½   teaspoon baking powder

½   cup packed basil leaves, finely chopped

1   small shallot, diced

6   ounces shredded part-skim mozzarella (about 1½ cups)

4   small slices crusty bread, such as baguette or sourdough, cut into ½-inch cubes (1½ cups)

1   Roma tomato, diced

INSTRUCTIONS:

1. Preheat the oven to 350°F.

2. Use a mixer to beat together the eggs, Greek yogurt, salt, pepper, spices, and baking powder until no clumps remain.

3. Whisk in the basil, shallot, and mozzarella.

4. Liberally grease a muffin pan with butter, olive oil, or nonstick spray. Put three or four pieces of bread in each tin (enough to cover the bottom). Top with a sprinkling of tomatoes. Scoop ¼ cup of the egg mixture into each tin. You want them to be just slightly more than three-quarters full, because if you fill them too high they will overflow when they bake.

5. Bake for 30 to 32 minutes, until the muffins are golden on top and a knife inserted in the center comes out clean. Let them cool in the pan for 5 minutes before sliding a knife around the edges of each muffin to loosen it, and then gently lift it out of the tin.

NUTRITION INFORMATION PER SERVING:
Calories 231, Calories from Fat 92, Fat (g) 10.2, Saturated Fat (g) 4.5, Protein (g) 18, Carbohydrate (g) 16.4, Dietary Fiber (g) 1.2, Cholesterol (mg) 233, Sodium (mg) 575

TEX-MEX SCRAMBLE FOR ONE

SERVES 1

Although I eat eggs in frittata and egg bake form, I'm not a big fan of scrambled eggs. When I want a savory scramble in the morning, I like creating flavorful dishes using vegetables, spices, and extra-firm tofu. This version combines green pepper, tomato, and red onion with the strong flavors of chili powder, cumin, and turmeric. To give it an extra Tex-Mex feel, I added corn tortilla strips and crumbled feta. This recipe serves one, but it is easily doubled. If you're serving someone who does not eat dairy, simply omit the feta.

INGREDIENTS:

2   teaspoons olive oil

1   clove garlic, minced

¼   cup chopped red onion

⅛   teaspoon sea salt (or to taste)

½   green pepper, diced

½   tomato, diced

3½ ounces extra-firm tofu, pressed and crumbled

½   tablespoon nutritional yeast

¼   teaspoon chili powder

¼   teaspoon cumin

⅛   teaspoon turmeric

1   small corn tortilla, cut into 1-inch pieces

2 tablespoons crumbled feta

Cilantro, for garnish

INSTRUCTIONS:

1. Heat the olive oil in a large nonstick skillet. Add the garlic and cook for 30 seconds, then stir in the onion and salt and cook for 2 to 3 minutes, until softened.

2. Stir in the green pepper, tomato, crumbled tofu, nutritional yeast, and spices. Cook for 4 to 5 minutes, stirring frequently, until the pepper is softened.

3. Remove the pan from the heat, and stir in the tortilla and feta. Transfer to a plate and top with cilantro.

NUTRITION INFORMATION PER SERVING:
Calories 355, Calories from Fat 189, Fat (g) 21, Saturated Fat (g) 4.9, Protein (g) 18.9, Carbohydrate (g) 28.2, Dietary Fiber (g) 5.2, Cholesterol (mg) 17, Sodium (mg) 556

QUINOA PANCAKES WITH RASPBERRY ORANGE SYRUP

If you've ever cooked with quinoa, you know how it soaks up and expands with the liquid around it—whether that be soup, sauce, dressing or, it turns out, pancake batter. Using quinoa flour gives these pancakes a light, fluffy texture, and packs them full of protein. Instead of purchasing quinoa flour at the store, which can be very expensive, I simply used a coffee grinder to pulverize the little seeds into a powder.

INGREDIENTS:

Quinoa Pancakes

½   cup dry quinoa (or ¾ cup quinoa flour)

¼   cup quick oats

½   tablespoon baking powder

1   teaspoon ground cinnamon

Pinch of salt

2   teaspoons coconut oil, melted

1   tablespoon dark brown sugar

½   cup fat-free Greek yogurt

¼   cup plus 2 tablespoons 2% milk

1   teaspoon vanilla extract

1   large egg, lightly beaten

Raspberry Orange Syrup

1   cup raspberries (frozen or fresh)

1½ tablespoons granulated sugar

¼   teaspoon orange zest

1½ tablespoons fresh-squeezed orange juice

1   teaspoon cornstarch

INSTRUCTIONS:

1. Place the quinoa in a coffee grinder. Grind until superfine—this will result in quinoa flour.

2. Whisk together the quinoa flour, oats, baking powder, cinnamon, and salt in a bowl.

3. In another bowl, combine the coconut oil, sugar, yogurt, milk, vanilla, and egg.

4. Gradually whisk the dry ingredients into the wet ingredients until combined.

5. Heat a griddle to 375°F. Coat with cooking spray. Spoon on ¼ cup of batter and cook until bubbles form and the edges begin to firm. Flip carefully and cook for another few minutes, until golden. Repeat with the remaining batter. This recipe will make six pancakes.

6. For the syrup, combine the raspberries, sugar, orange zest and juice, and cornstarch in a medium saucepan. As the sauce heats up, smash the raspberries with a spoon. Bring to a boil, and reduce to simmer for 3 to 5 minutes without a cover, until slightly thickened.

7. Serve the pancakes with warm syrup.

NUTRITION INFORMATION PER SERVING:

Calories 443, Calories from Fat 103, Fat (g) 11.5, Saturated Fat (g) 5.7, Protein (g) 18.5, Carbohydrate (g) 68.1, Dietary Fiber (g) 8.7, Cholesterol (mg) 98, Sodium (mg) 435

PEANUT BUTTER AND BANANA BAKED OATMEAL

SERVES 4

I eat oatmeal nearly every day for breakfast, and usually love it, but my standby bowl of oats can quickly become boring. Baked oatmeal is a great alternative to the microwaved oatmeal routine. This version has all the warm flavors of banana bread, with texture from hearty old-fashioned oats, a creamy splash of low-fat milk, and a dab of protein-packed peanut butter. To keep this breakfast convenient, I like making a batch of it on Sunday, and reheating it before work during the week.

INGREDIENTS:

1½ cups old-fashioned oats

1   teaspoon ground cinnamon

¼   teaspoon ground nutmeg

½   teaspoon baking powder

⅛   teaspoon salt

2   medium overripe bananas

⅓   cup creamy peanut butter

1   cup 1% milk

3   tablespoons maple syrup

½   tablespoon vanilla extract

1   egg, or 1 "flax egg" (1 tablespoon ground flaxseed mixed with 3 tablespoons warm water)

INSTRUCTIONS:

1. Preheat the oven to 375°F.

2. Combine the oats, cinnamon, nutmeg, baking powder, and salt in a bowl. Set aside.

3. In another bowl, mash the bananas well, then whisk in the peanut butter, milk, maple syrup, vanilla, and egg or flax egg.

4. Whisk the dry ingredients into the wet ingredients until well combined. Pour into an 8 x 8-inch baking dish coated with nonstick spray.

5. Bake for 35 to 40 minutes, until golden on top and set.

6. Let sit for a few minutes, then slice into four pieces and serve warm with additional milk, or topped with a dollop of Greek yogurt, if desired.

NUTRITION INFORMATION PER SERVING:
Calories 378, Calories from Fat 128, Fat (g) 14.2, Saturated Fat (g) 2.2, Protein (g) 12.4, Carbohydrate (g) 53.4, Dietary Fiber (g) 6.8, Cholesterol (mg) 3, Sodium (mg) 233

ROASTED STRAWBERRY AND PEANUT BUTTER BREAKFAST QUESADILLA

SERVES 2

Peanut butter and jelly toast makes its way into my weekday routine more often than I like to admit. Sometimes I just crave that sweet, salty, rich taste of childhood. These quesadillas take that flavor profile to the next level, with a creamy peanut butter spread made with protein-rich Greek yogurt and lightly sweet mascarpone cheese, and topped with juicy roasted strawberries.

INGREDIENTS:

5   medium-sized strawberries, thinly sliced

1   teaspoon granulated sugar

½   teaspoon vanilla extract, divided

⅓   cup plain nonfat Greek yogurt

¼   cup natural creamy peanut butter

1   tablespoon mascarpone cheese

1   teaspoon loosely packed dark brown sugar

¼   teaspoon ground cinnamon

2   whole wheat flour tortillas

INSTRUCTIONS:

1. Preheat the oven to 375°F.

2. Stir together the strawberries, granulated sugar, and half of the vanilla. Place on a parchment-lined baking sheet, and roast for 15 minutes.

3. Combine the yogurt, peanut butter, mascarpone, brown sugar, and cinnamon with the remaining vanilla in a food processor. Process until everything is whipped together.

4. Spread half of the peanut butter on half of one tortilla. Top with half of the strawberries, then fold the other half of the tortilla over the top. Press down so it sticks together. Repeat with remaining tortilla and ingredients.

5. Coat a nonstick pan with cooking spray (I like coconut oil cooking spray for this). Brown the quesadillas for about 3 minutes on medium heat on each side, until golden.

6. Serve as is or with a little drizzle of honey.

NUTRITION INFORMATION PER SERVING:
Calories 381, Calories from Fat 180, Fat (g) 20, Saturated Fat (g) 4.1, Protein (g) 16.4, Carbohydrate (g) 37.4, Dietary Fiber (g) 5.6, Cholesterol (mg) 12, Sodium (mg) 335

CARROT CAKE WAFFLES WITH MAPLE CREAM CHEESE GLAZE

SERVES 2

You don't need to feel naughty about indulging in these fluffy carrot cake waffles. Each serving of these lightly sweetened waffles boasts 20 grams of protein and loads of vitamin A. The whole wheat flour and oats make these super filling, while the maple cream cheese glaze adds decadence to the most important meal of the day.

INGREDIENTS:

⅔ cup 2% plain Greek yogurt

3 tablespoons 2% milk

½ tablespoon vanilla extract

1 tablespoon packed dark brown sugar

1 large egg, lightly beaten

½ cup peeled and finely grated carrot (about ¾ regular-sized carrot)

½ cup white whole wheat flour

½ cup quick oats

¾ teaspoon baking powder

⅛ teaspoon salt

¾ teaspoon ground cinnamon

½ teaspoon ground nutmeg

¼ teaspoon ground ginger

Maple Cream Cheese Glaze

2 ounces light cream cheese

2½ tablespoons maple syrup

INSTRUCTIONS:

1. Preheat your waffle iron.

2. Whisk together the yogurt, milk, vanilla, and brown sugar until smooth. Whisk in the egg, and then the carrot.

3. In a separate bowl, combine together the flour, oats, baking powder, salt, cinnamon, nutmeg, and ginger.

4. Use a fork to stir the dry ingredients into the wet ingredients until just combined.

5. Coat your waffle iron with nonstick spray, then scoop the batter onto the waffle plates. Cook the waffles according to your waffle iron's instructions. The recipe will make four deep-pocket waffles.

6. While the waffles are cooking, heat the cream cheese and maple syrup in the microwave for 10 to 15 seconds. Transfer to a food processor or blender, and pulse a few times until smooth.

7. Divide the glaze among the cooked waffles.

NUTRITION INFORMATION PER SERVING:
Calories 464, Calories from Fat 106, Fat (g) 11.8, Saturated Fat (g) 6, Protein (g) 20.5, Carbohydrate (g) 72.1, Dietary Fiber (g) 9.8, Cholesterol (mg) 114, Sodium (mg) 471

FLUFFY BANANA BREAD PANCAKES

SERVES 2

I'm not exaggerating when I say I tested this recipe seven times before I got it just right. The recipe below makes fluffy pancakes with the warm spices and sweetness of banana bread. They're also packed with protein from Greek yogurt, whole wheat pastry flour, and oats. I like topping mine with extra bananas and maple syrup, or warm, melted peanut butter drizzle. If you want something extra sweet, sprinkle a few teaspoons of mini semisweet chocolate chips on each pancake while the first side is cooking.

INGREDIENTS:

1   large ripe banana, mashed

½   cup 2% plain Greek yogurt

3   tablespoons 1% buttermilk

1   tablespoon packed dark brown sugar

2   teaspoons vanilla extract

1   large egg, beaten

¼   cup quick (1-minute) oats

½   cup whole wheat pastry flour

1   teaspoon baking powder

½   teaspoon ground cinnamon

¼   teaspoon ground nutmeg

⅛   teaspoon fine sea salt

INSTRUCTIONS:

1. Preheat a griddle to 375°F.

2. Whisk together the mashed banana, Greek yogurt, buttermilk, sugar, vanilla, and egg. Stir in the oats. Set aside.

3. In another bowl, sift together the flour, baking powder, cinnamon, nutmeg, and salt.

4. Gradually add the wet ingredients to the dry ingredients, using a fork or spoon to mix the batter. Do not use a mixer, because you could overmix the batter. Stop mixing when the mixture is combined.

5. Scoop ¼ cup of batter onto a griddle coated with cooking spray. After the corners start to firm and you see bubbles break on top, carefully flip the pancake. Cook on the remaining side until golden (usually about 3 minutes). Repeat with the remaining batter. This recipe will make six pancakes.

NUTRITION INFORMATION PER SERVING:
Calories 340, Calories from Fat 47, Fat (g) 5.2, Saturated Fat (g) 1.9, Protein (g) 14.7, Carbohydrate (g) 57.5, Dietary Fiber (g) 7.2, Cholesterol (mg) 97, Sodium (mg) 422

ALMOND CINNAMON ROLLS WITH GREEK YOGURT GLAZE

SERVES 8

Eating a cinnamon roll for breakfast doesn't have to mean lacking in the protein department! These rolls have 10 grams of protein and are made with whole grains, which will help keep you full for hours. They're fluffy, comforting, indulgent, and totally worth waking up a bit early on a cozy weekend morning.

INGREDIENTS:

Almond Butter Sweet Roll Dough

¾   cup 1% milk

2   tablespoons unsalted butter, cut into chunks

¼   cup creamy natural unsalted almond butter

1¾ cups whole wheat pastry flour

1¼ cups unbleached all-purpose flour, divided

1   package (2¼ teaspoons) quick-rise or instant yeast

2   tablespoons packed dark brown sugar

¼   teaspoon salt

½   teaspoon baking powder

1   teaspoon almond extract

1   large egg

⅓   cup sliced almonds

INSTRUCTIONS:

1. Heat the milk in a small saucepan over medium heat just until it starts to bubble on top. Remove from the heat and whisk in the butter and almond butter until melted. Set aside and let cool to a lukewarm temperature while you get the dry ingredients together.

2. In a large mixing bowl, whisk together the whole wheat pastry flour, ¼ cup of the all-purpose flour, yeast, brown sugar, salt, and baking powder. Beat in the almond extract, egg, and the lukewarm milk mixture.

3. Add the remaining flour ¼ cup at a time, mixing well after each addition. Once you have a loose dough, either use a kneading hook in your mixer for about 3 minutes, or knead on a floured surface until smooth (about 5 minutes). The dough will be *very* sticky. If you're kneading, add flour as needed so it doesn't stick to your hands or the surface. After you knead for a minute or two, it will become easier to handle.

4. Cover the dough with a damp towel and let it rest for 30 minutes, until it holds its shape when poked.

5. While the dough is rising, combine the butter, brown sugar, cinnamon, and vanilla for the filling.

Brown Sugar Cinnamon Filling

6   tablespoons butter, softened

1   cup packed dark brown sugar

1   tablespoon ground cinnamon

1   teaspoon vanilla extract

Glaze

¼–⅓ cup powdered sugar (depending on desired thickness)

¼   teaspoon vanilla extract

⅓   cup plus 2 tablespoons 2% plain Greek yogurt

6. Use a rolling pin to create a 12 x 10-inch rectangle with the dough. Cover the entire dough surface with the filling mixture. Carefully roll up the dough. Pinch the seam to seal. Cut off the end pieces, and then cut the remaining dough into eight rolls. It's easiest to do this with a very sharp knife, lightly sawing back and forth. Place the rolls cut-side up in a greased 9-inch cake or pie pan, cover with a damp towel, and let rise for another 45 minutes. Set the oven to preheat to 375°F.

7. After the dough has risen, put the rolls in the oven for 20 to 25 minutes. Check them after 20 minutes, and if they're not quite done, but are getting brown on top, cover them with aluminum foil for the last few minutes.

8. While the rolls are baking, combine the powdered sugar, vanilla, and yogurt in a bowl for the glaze. Whisk until smooth.

9. Sprinkle the almonds and drizzle the glaze on top of the warm rolls. Only frost the ones you're eating right away, then store the unglazed rolls in an airtight container at room temperature, and keep the glaze in the fridge. When you're ready to eat, sprinkle a roll with almonds and drizzle with icing, then warm briefly in the microwave.

NUTRITION INFORMATION PER SERVING:

Calories 510, Calories from Fat 178, Fat (g) 19.8, Saturated Fat (g) 8.4, Protein (g) 10.7, Carbohydrate (g) 74.2, Dietary Fiber (g) 5.8, Cholesterol (mg) 56, Sodium (mg) 132

CHAPTER TWO

SOUPS, SALADS, AND GRAINS

CHUNKY POTATO AND LENTIL SOUP

SERVES 6

I fell in love with lentil soup several years ago. At that time I just devoured the canned version, but I've now learned that it's easy to make at home and customize to your own tastes. This version combines celery, carrots, and potatoes with a super-flavorful tomato-lentil base. I love serving this soup with a dollop of sour cream, a sprinkle of Parmesan, and a handful of crispy tortilla chips for dipping.

INGREDIENTS:

2   tablespoons unsalted butter

3   cloves garlic, minced

2   shallots, sliced

3   stalks celery, chopped

2   large carrots, peeled and finely chopped

2   russet potatoes, peeled and chopped into ½-inch cubes

2   teaspoons garbanzo bean flour (or unbleached all-purpose flour)

1   cup water

4   cups vegetable broth

1   (28-ounce) can no-salt-added diced tomatoes

2   cups French green lentils, picked over and rinsed

1   teaspoon ground cumin

1   teaspoon dried oregano

⅛–¼ teaspoon fine sea salt, or to taste

¼   teaspoon ground white pepper

½   teaspoon red pepper flakes

2   bay leaves

1   tablespoon Dijon mustard

INSTRUCTIONS:

1. Heat the butter in a large pot over medium-low heat. Stir in the garlic and cook for 30 seconds, and then add the shallots and cook for 2 to 3 minutes, until translucent and soft.

2. Pour in the celery, carrots, and potatoes. Cook for about 10 minutes, until all of the vegetables are softened.

3. Whisk the flour into the water until fully dissolved. Add the flour-water mixture, vegetable broth, tomatoes, lentils, spices, and bay leaves into the pot. Reduce the heat to low, cover, and simmer for 45 minutes.

4. Remove bay leaves from the soup, then stir in the Dijon mustard.

5. Serve with Parmesan cheese, sour cream, and tortilla chips.

NUTRITION INFORMATION PER SERVING:
Calories 356, Calories from Fat 46, Fat (g) 5.1, Saturated Fat (g) 2.6, Protein (g) 19.3, Carbohydrate (g) 61.8, Dietary Fiber (g) 18, Cholesterol (mg) 10, Sodium (mg) 846

TOMATO BARLEY WHITE BEAN SOUP

SERVES 5

Tomato soup always reminds me of winter nights of my childhood. On especially chilly evenings, my mom would make a hearty tomato soup and buttery cheddar biscuits to help warm up my siblings and me. This higher-protein twist on my mother's recipe combines sun-dried tomatoes, crushed tomatoes, and fire-roasted tomatoes with plump pearl barley and navy beans. It's comforting, flavorful, and sure to make those chilly winter nights a little more bearable.

INGREDIENTS:

- 3 tablespoons olive oil
- 3 cloves garlic, minced
- ½ yellow onion, chopped
- ½ cup sun-dried tomato halves, chopped
- 1 tablespoon unbleached all-purpose flour
- 1 tablespoon water
- 1 (28-ounce) can no-salt-added crushed tomatoes
- 1 (28-ounce) can fire-roasted diced tomatoes
- 2 cups vegetable broth
- 1 cup 2% milk
- 2 tablespoons herbes de Provence
- 1 tablespoon dried rosemary
- ½ teaspoon ground white pepper
- ¼ teaspoon ground black pepper
- ¼ teaspoon crushed red pepper
- ⅛–¼ teaspoon fine sea salt (or to taste)
- 2 teaspoons granulated sugar
- 1 (15-ounce) can no-salt-added navy beans, rinsed and drained
- 1 cup pearl barley

INSTRUCTIONS:

1. Heat the olive oil over medium heat in a large saucepan. Add the garlic and cook for 30 seconds. Pour in the onion and cook until translucent, 2 to 3 minutes.

2. Add the sun-dried tomatoes to the pan and cook for another 2 to 3 minutes, until softened.

3. Whisk together the flour and water. Add the flour mixture, crushed tomatoes, diced tomatoes, broth, milk, spices, sugar, beans, and barley to the soup pot. Taste and adjust the seasonings to your liking. Cover and simmer on low for 25 to 30 minutes, until the barley is tender.

NUTRITION INFORMATION PER SERVING:
Calories 431, Calories from Fat 93, Fat (g) 10.4, Saturated Fat (g) 2.1, Protein (g) 14.7, Carbohydrate (g) 70.9, Dietary Fiber (g) 17.5, Cholesterol (mg) 4, Sodium (mg) 748

CUBAN BLACK BEAN SOUP

SERVES 5

This soup comes together quickly, and packs tons of flavor with black beans, lime, and Cuban-inspired spices. Pureeing half of the batch results in a thick, creamy soup that still has great texture. The recipe can easily be doubled; you then freeze the leftovers for those weeks when you need easy, healthy meals.

INGREDIENTS:

2   tablespoons canola oil

3   cloves garlic, minced

1   small red onion, diced

¼–½ teaspoon fine sea salt, or to taste, divided

1   red bell pepper, diced

3   cups vegetable broth

3   (15-ounce) cans no-salt-added black beans, drained and rinsed

Juice of 1 lime

½   teaspoon ground black pepper

1   bay leaf

1   tablespoon ground cumin

1   tablespoon dried Mexican oregano

1½ teaspoons paprika

¼–½ teaspoon red pepper flakes

¼   teaspoon ground turmeric

1   avocado, cubed, for topping

INSTRUCTIONS:

1. Heat the oil over medium heat in a large pot, then add the garlic cloves. Cook for 30 seconds.

2. Add the onion and half of the salt. Cook for a few minutes, until the onion is soft.

3. Add the red pepper to the pan and cook for another 5 minutes, stirring frequently, until it has softened.

4. Pour in the broth, beans, lime juice, remaining salt, pepper, bay leaf, and all of the spices. Cover and simmer for 30 minutes.

5. Remove the bay leaf, transfer half of the soup to a food processor or blender, and blend until smooth. Pour the pureed soup back into the soup pot.

6. Divide the soup among five bowls, and top with avocado. I also love this soup with sour cream, cilantro, and corn chips on the side.

NUTRITION INFORMATION PER SERVING:
Calories 353, Calories from Fat 101, Fat (g) 11.2, Saturated Fat (g) 1.3, Protein (g) 14.9, Carbohydrate (g) 51.8, Dietary Fiber (g) 12.6, Cholesterol (mg) 0, Sodium (mg) 697

ROASTED RED PEPPER, CORN, AND COUSCOUS BISQUE

SERVES 5

Roasted red pepper and tomato bisque is one of my all-time favorite comfort foods. The creamy, thick soup is absolutely perfect for chilly nights at home. Instead of heavy cream (which is used in most bisque recipes), this soup's creaminess comes from pureed roasted corn and reduced-fat milk. Since I like texture in my soup, I added protein-packed whole wheat couscous after pureeing the soup. The couscous not only adds protein and fiber, but also makes the soup extra satisfying.

INGREDIENTS

3 cups frozen corn kernels

3 tablespoons olive oil, divided

2 cloves garlic, minced

1 yellow onion, roughly chopped

½ teaspoon fine sea salt, or to taste

1 (11.5-ounce) jar roasted red peppers, drained, rinsed, and roughly chopped

1 (28-ounce) can no-salt-added crushed tomatoes

1 cup vegetable broth

½ tablespoon dried rosemary

¼ teaspoon crushed red pepper

2 cups 2% milk

1⅓ cups whole wheat couscous

2 cups warm water

INSTRUCTIONS:

1. Preheat the oven to 450°F.

2. Toss the corn with 2 tablespoons of the olive oil, and place on a baking sheet. Roast for 10 to 12 minutes, until just very lightly browned. Set aside ¼ cup of the kernels for garnish.

3. Heat the remaining olive oil in a large pot. Add the garlic and cook for 30 seconds. Pour in the onion and the salt, and cook for a few minutes, until softened.

4. Add the corn (minus the ¼ cup for garnish), roasted red peppers, tomatoes, broth, rosemary, crushed red pepper, and milk. Bring to a boil, then cover and simmer for 20 minutes.

5. Use an immersion blender, or transfer the soup to a food processor, and process until smooth.

6. Pour the pureed soup back in the pot and bring to a boil. Stir in the couscous. Cover and remove from heat, and let sit for 5 minutes.

7. The couscous will soak up liquid and make the soup very thick. You may eat as is, but I like to thin it out with 2 cups of water.

8. Divide into bowls, and top with additional corn kernels.

NUTRITION INFORMATION PER SERVING:
Calories 412, Calories from Fat 112, Fat (g) 12.4, Saturated Fat (g) 2.5, Protein (g) 13.7, Carbohydrate (g) 68.2, Dietary Fiber (g) 7.7, Cholesterol (mg) 8, Sodium (mg) 681

CAPRESE PESTO KALE SALAD WITH CRISPY TOFU

SERVES 4

This salad is not only easy to make but also packed with protein, nutrients, and Italian flavors. Bites of fresh mozzarella are mixed with sweet cherry tomatoes, baby kale, tofu crispy enough to be mistaken for croutons, and a flavorful basil pesto dressing.

INGREDIENTS:

Caprese Salad with Crispy Tofu

1 (14-ounce) container extra-firm tofu

3 tablespoons extra-virgin olive oil

½ teaspoon fine sea salt

2 cups cherry tomatoes, measured whole then sliced in half

6 ounces fresh mozzarella balls, sliced in half (about ½ cup)

2 cups packed baby kale

Basil Pesto Dressing

2 cups packed fresh basil leaves

2 cloves garlic

¼ teaspoon fine sea salt

2 tablespoons pine nuts

½ cup low-sodium vegetable broth

2 tablespoons extra-virgin olive oil

INSTRUCTIONS:

1. Slice the tofu into four pieces. Wrap the pieces in a towel, place a cutting board on top of the towel, and press down with all your body weight. Do this three or four times. Cut the tofu into cubes.

2. Heat the olive oil in a large nonstick skillet over medium heat. Add the tofu and salt, and cook, stirring occasionally, until all sides are golden brown (10 to 15 minutes).

3. While the tofu is cooking, make the pesto: Combine the basil, garlic, salt, and pine nuts in a food processor. Pulse until all ingredients are very finely chopped. Slowly pour in the vegetable broth while the processor is running, and then add the olive oil, again while the processor is running.

4. Combine the tomatoes, mozzarella, fried tofu, and kale in a large bowl. Stir in the pesto dressing.

NUTRITION INFORMATION PER SERVING (¼ OF SALAD):
Calories 327, Calories from Fat 237, Fat (g) 26.3, Saturated Fat (g) 5, Protein (g) 20.8, Carbohydrate (g) 8.1, Dietary Fiber (g) 2, Cholesterol (mg) 15, Sodium (mg) 351

NUTRITION INFORMATION PER SERVING (¼ OF DRESSING):
Calories 100, Calories from Fat 89, Fat (g) 9.9, Saturated Fat (g) 1.2, Protein (g) 1.2, Carbohydrate (g) 2.5, Dietary Fiber (g) 1, Cholesterol (mg) 0, Sodium (mg) 179

SHREDDED BRUSSELS SPROUT SALAD WITH ORZO AND LEMON SHALLOT DRESSING

SERVES 5

If you like loads of texture in your meals, you will love this salad! Al dente orzo pasta is mixed with crunchy shredded brussels sprouts, slivered almonds, sweet-yet-tart cranberries, and creamy goat cheese. The lemon dressing is tangy, fresh, lightly sweet, and the perfect complement to the flavorful salad. It's easy to throw together, full of good-for-you ingredients, and can be made ahead of time. In fact, it tastes even better after the flavors come together in the fridge overnight.

INGREDIENTS:

Brussels Sprout Salad with Orzo

1   cup orzo

6   cups shredded brussels sprouts

⅓   cup slivered almonds

½   cup dried cranberries

4   ounces crumbled goat cheese

Lemon Shallot Dressing

1   shallot, chopped

1   clove garlic

½   tablespoon fresh thyme leaves

Juice of 1 lemon

¼   teaspoon lemon zest

½   tablespoon honey

¾   teaspoon fine sea salt, or to taste

¼   teaspoon ground black pepper, or to taste

¼   cup olive oil

INSTRUCTIONS:

1. Cook the orzo according to the package instructions. Mine took about 9 minutes until it was al dente. Drain, rinse in cold water, and set aside in a large bowl to cool completely.

2. Once the orzo cools to room temperature, stir in the brussels sprouts, almonds, cranberries, and goat cheese.

3. Combine all of the dressing ingredients, except the olive oil, in a food processor. Pulse until smooth, and then pour in the olive oil while the processor is running.

4. Pour the dressing into the salad and mix well. The salad can be eaten immediately, but the flavor will improve if it sits overnight in the refrigerator.

NUTRITION INFORMATION PER SERVING:
Calories 434, Calories from Fat 186, Fat (g) 20.7, Saturated Fat (g) 5.3, Protein (g) 13.9, Carbohydrate (g) 51.9, Dietary Fiber (g) 5.9, Cholesterol (mg) 10, Sodium (mg) 395

THREE-BEAN QUINOA TACO SALAD

SERVES 6

Quinoa salads are one of my favorite weekday lunches because they keep well throughout the week. The quinoa and beans provide protein, while the romaine and avocado add crunch and creaminess. The Cilantro Lime Vinaigrette elevates all the flavors in the salad, and adds tanginess and extra freshness.

INGREDIENTS:

Three-Bean Quinoa Salad

1   cup quinoa

2   cups vegetable broth

1   cup black beans, drained and rinsed

1   cup white kidney beans, drained and rinsed

1   cup garbanzo beans, drained and rinsed

2   Roma tomatoes, diced

4   cups chopped romaine (about 6 ounces)

½   cup cilantro, chopped (plus more for garnish)

1   avocado, cubed

Cilantro Lime Vinaigrette

¼   cup fresh cilantro

¼   yellow onion, chopped

1   Roma tomato, seeded and chopped

1   tablespoon white wine vinegar

Juice of 1 lime

2   cloves garlic

1   teaspoon dried oregano

¼   teaspoon fine sea salt

¼   teaspoon ground black pepper

½   teaspoon ground cumin

¼   teaspoon paprika

2½ tablespoons olive oil

INSTRUCTIONS:

1. Combine the quinoa and vegetable broth in a medium-sized pot over medium heat. Bring to a boil, then cover and reduce to a simmer for 15 to 20 minutes, until all the liquid is absorbed.

2. While the quinoa cooks, get the dressing together: Combine all of the ingredients except the olive oil in a food processor. Process until very finely chopped. Slowly drizzle in the olive oil with the processor running.

3. Combine the cooked quinoa, beans, tomatoes, romaine, and cilantro in a large bowl. Pour in the dressing and toss thoroughly.

4. Divide into six bowls, and top with avocado and additional cilantro. Only add the avocado immediately before serving.

NUTRITION INFORMATION PER SERVING:
Calories 338, Calories from Fat 110, Fat (g) 12.3, Saturated Fat (g) 1.7, Protein (g) 12.8, Carbohydrate (g) 47.1, Dietary Fiber (g) 11.4, Cholesterol (mg) 0, Sodium (mg) 632

FRESH VEGGIE QUINOA SALAD WITH LEMON TAHINI DRESSING

SERVES 5

Eating your veggies should never mean eating a boring salad. This quinoa salad is crazy colorful and full of flavor from tomatoes, red pepper, zucchini, and a simple Lemon Tahini Dressing. The flavor improves overnight, so this is a perfect make-ahead meal. I like the crunch and color of the raw red onions, but if you're not a fan, simply add all of the chopped onion to the pot with the garlic.

INGREDIENTS:

Quinoa Salad

½   tablespoon olive oil

2   cloves garlic, minced

½   red onion, chopped, divided

1   cup quinoa (I used tricolor quinoa)

2   cups water

½   teaspoon kosher salt

3   tablespoons chopped fresh thyme

1   zucchini, diced

1   red pepper, diced

1   tomato, diced

1   (15-ounce) can chickpeas, rinsed and drained

½   cup unsalted slivered raw almonds, toasted if desired

Lemon Tahini Dressing

¼   cup tahini (sesame seed paste)

¼   cup water

¼   cup lemon juice

1   clove garlic

¼   teaspoon kosher salt

⅛   teaspoon freshly ground pepper

½   tablespoon olive oil

INSTRUCTIONS:

1. Heat the olive oil over medium heat in a large saucepan. Cook the garlic in the oil until fragrant (about a minute).

2. Add half of the onion and cook until translucent. Pour in the quinoa and toast for 2 to 3 minutes, then add the water, salt, and thyme. Bring to a boil, then reduce the heat to low, cover, and let simmer for 15 minutes.

3. For the dressing, pulse the tahini, water, lemon, garlic, salt, and pepper in a food processor until smooth. Slowly add the olive oil while the processor is running.

4. Add the chopped vegetables (including the remaining raw red onion), chickpeas, and almonds to the cooked quinoa, then pour the dressing over the mixture. Stir well and serve.

NUTRITION INFORMATION PER SERVING:

Calories 422, Calories from Fat 172, Fat (g) 19.1, Saturated Fat (g) 2.2, Protein (g) 15.9, Carbohydrate (g) 51.5, Dietary Fiber (g) 11.3, Cholesterol (mg) 0, Sodium (mg) 222

ASIAN PEANUT BROCCOLI QUINOA

SERVES 5

Nothing makes me gobble up my veggies faster than a sweet, salty, and protein-packed peanut butter sauce. This version combines peanut butter with soy sauce, dark brown sugar, honey, tomato paste, spicy red pepper flakes, and a touch of ginger. The addictive sauce goes over high-protein quinoa, crispy pan-fried tofu, and sautéed broccoli. Top each bowl with some crushed peanuts for extra crunch, and you'll not only be devouring those veggies, but you'll have a healthy, protein-filled meal that'll keep you full for hours.

INGREDIENTS:

1¼ cups quinoa

2½ cups water

¼ cup reduced-sodium soy sauce

1½ tablespoons peanut butter

1 tablespoon tomato paste

⅛ teaspoon freshly grated gingerroot

1 tablespoon dark brown sugar

1 tablespoon honey

1 teaspoon brown rice vinegar

⅛ teaspoon crushed red pepper

2 tablespoons peanut oil

3 green onions, chopped, divided

⅛ teaspoon fine sea salt

1 (14-ounce) container extra-firm tofu, cut into ½-inch cubes

2 broccoli stalks, chopped (about 3 cups)

5 tablespoons finely chopped unsalted peanuts

INSTRUCTIONS:

1. Combine the quinoa and water in a medium-sized pot over medium heat. Bring to a boil, then cover and reduce to a simmer for 15 to 20 minutes, until all the liquid is absorbed.

2. Whisk together the soy sauce, peanut butter, tomato paste, ginger, brown sugar, honey, brown rice vinegar, and crushed red pepper. Set aside.

3. Heat the oil in a large nonstick skillet over medium heat. Add the white pieces of the chopped green onions and salt, and cook for 2 to 3 minutes, until softened. Add the tofu and cook for 10 to 15 minutes, until browned on all sides. Add the broccoli to the pan and cook for an additional 3 to 5 minutes, until the broccoli is bright green and slightly softened. Remove from the heat.

4. Pour the cooked quinoa into the tofu-broccoli mixture, then mix in the soy/peanut sauce.

5. Divide into five bowls. Garnish with the green section of green onions, and a sprinkle of finely chopped peanuts.

NUTRITION INFORMATION PER SERVING:
Calories 437, Calories from Fat 188, Fat (g) 20.9, Saturated Fat (g) 2.7, Protein (g) 21.6, Carbohydrate (g) 46.1, Dietary Fiber (g) 6.4, Cholesterol (mg) 0, Sodium (mg) 577

RED LENTIL COCONUT CURRY

SERVES 4

Red curry is one of those flavors that I wake up in the middle of the night craving. There's something amazingly addictive about it to me. When I realized I could make it at home, I knew my life had changed for the better. This version is high in protein from the red lentils, which break down into a thick, coconut-spiked red curry sauce. The meal is perfect as is, just served over long-grain brown rice (I recommend jasmine or basmati), but you can also add some of your favorite vegetables—stir-fried broccoli and red pepper would be delicious.

INGREDIENTS:

- 1   tablespoon coconut oil
- 1   clove garlic, minced
- 1   shallot, diced
- 1   cup split red lentils, picked through and rinsed
- 1   (15-ounce) can light coconut milk
- 1   cup water
- 2   tablespoons red curry paste
- ½   teaspoon curry powder
- ¼   teaspoon turmeric
- ¼   teaspoon ground ginger
- ½   teaspoon ground cumin
- ⅛–¼ teaspoon ground cayenne
- ¼–½ teaspoon fine sea salt, or to taste
- Juice of ½ small lemon
- 1   cup long-grain brown rice (jasmine or basmati recommended)
- 1   tablespoon butter (optional)
- Cilantro, for garnish

INSTRUCTIONS:

1. Melt the coconut oil in a medium-sized saucepan. Add the garlic and cook for 30 seconds, then add the shallot and cook for 2 to 3 minutes, until translucent and softened.

2. Pour in the lentils, coconut milk, and water. Bring to a boil, then reduce the heat to low, cover, and simmer for 10 minutes, stirring occasionally.

3. After 10 minutes, remove the cover and add the curry paste, all spices, and lemon juice. Let simmer uncovered for 15 to 20 minutes, stirring frequently, until thickened. You want it thick enough that you see the bottom of the pan when you stir.

4. While the lentils simmer, cook the rice in lightly salted water according to the package directions (this will vary depending on the type of rice you use).

5. If desired, stir the butter into the cooked rice.

6. Divide the rice among four plates, and top each plate with a quarter of the lentils. Garnish with cilantro.

NUTRITION INFORMATION PER SERVING:
Calories 467, Calories from Fat 95, Fat (g) 10.5, Saturated Fat (g) 7.7, Protein (g) 16.6, Carbohydrate (g) 76.2, Dietary Fiber (g) 16, Cholesterol (mg) 0, Sodium (mg) 485

SESAME SOY LETTUCE WRAPS

SERVES 5

There's something so satisfying about the hot and cold crunch of lettuce wraps. These wraps are filled with long-grain brown rice that's cooked with a hint of coconut and lime, and then topped with a hearty sesame and soy vegetable stir-fry. Lettuce wraps are traditionally served with iceberg lettuce, but I like to serve mine in romaine leaves for a little extra health boost. You could serve these as an appetizer, but they're so filling and satisfying that we usually eat them as a main entrée.

INGREDIENTS:

Coconut Lime Rice

1 cup brown jasmine rice

⅛ teaspoon fine sea salt

1¼ cups water

½ cup light coconut milk

Juice of 1 lime

½ tablespoon toasted sesame oil

Sesame Soy Filling

2 cloves garlic, minced

2½ tablespoons reduced-sodium soy sauce

¼ cup brown rice vinegar

2 tablespoons honey

1 teaspoon freshly grated gingerroot

¼ teaspoon crushed red pepper flakes

Juice of 1 lime

3 tablespoons toasted sesame oil, divided

3 green onions, sliced

8 ounces tempeh, sliced into ½-inch cubes

INSTRUCTIONS:

1. Bring the rice, salt, water, coconut milk, and lime to a boil. Cover, reduce the heat to low, and simmer for 30 minutes. Remove from the heat (with the cover on) and set aside for 10 minutes. Add the toasted sesame oil and fluff with a fork. Note: If you are using a different variety of brown rice (other than jasmine), check the cooking instructions, as directions may vary.

2. Whisk together the garlic, soy sauce, vinegar, honey, ginger, red pepper flakes, lime juice, and 1½ tablespoons of the oil in a large bowl. Set aside.

3. In a large skillet, heat the remaining sesame oil. Add the onions and cook until softened.

4. Stir in the tempeh and cook for 5 to 7 minutes, until lightly browned. Pour in the mushrooms, red peppers, water chestnuts, and the ginger soy sauce. Cook, stirring occasionally, for 5 minutes, until the ingredients have absorbed most of the liquid. Sprinkle on the sesame seeds.

INGREDIENTS (continued):

4　ounces mushrooms, roughly chopped

2　roasted red peppers, chopped

1　(8-ounce) can water chestnuts, drained, rinsed, and chopped

1　tablespoon raw sesame seeds

Romaine, iceberg, or Bibb lettuce, for serving

Additional lime wedges, for serving

INSTRUCTIONS (continued):

5.　The amount of filling that fits in each wrap will depend on the size of the lettuce leaves you're using. Fill each leaf with rice, then the tempeh filling, and serve with additional lime wedges.

NUTRITION INFORMATION PER SERVING:

Calories 409, Calories from Fat 146, Fat (g) 16.2, Saturated Fat (g) 3.1, Protein (g) 14.8, Carbohydrate (g) 51.9, Dietary Fiber (g) 4.3, Cholesterol (mg) 0, Sodium (mg) 394

CHIPOTLE PEPPER, BEAN, AND WHEAT BERRY CHILI

SERVES 8

I once had a co-worker tell me I couldn't eat chili, because chili is always made with meat. This spicy, smoky (and vegetarian) chili might even convince my meat-loving colleague to try a meat-free version! I love making a batch of this on Sundays, and then having a quick, healthy, and totally comforting dinner ready to eat for the remainder of the week. Top with a sprinkle of sharp cheddar, a dollop of sour cream, and a side of crunchy corn tortilla chips for a satisfying cold-weather meal.

INGREDIENTS

½   cup wheat berries

1½ cups water

3   tablespoons olive oil

2   cloves garlic, minced

1   small red onion, diced

½–1 (7.5-ounce) can chipotle peppers in adobo sauce

3   celery stalks, chopped

1   green pepper, diced

1   red pepper, diced

4   cups vegetable stock

1   (28-ounce) can diced tomatoes

1   (24-ounce) jar strained tomatoes or tomato puree

⅛   teaspoon kosher salt, or to taste

¼   teaspoon black pepper

1   tablespoon chili powder

2   teaspoons cumin

½   tablespoon dried oregano

1   (15-ounce) can no-salt-added pinto beans, drained and rinsed

INSTRUCTIONS:

1. In a medium-sized saucepan, bring the wheat berries and water to a boil. Cover, reduce the heat to low, and simmer for an hour.

2. Heat the oil and garlic in a large saucepan. After about 30 seconds, the garlic will be fragrant. Add the onion and cook until translucent, about 3 minutes.

3. Drain the can of chipotle peppers in adobo sauce, reserving a couple of tablespoons of the liquid for use later. Cut the peppers in half, use a spoon to scoop out the seeds, and then roughly chop the peppers.

4. Add the celery, green peppers, red peppers, and chopped chipotle peppers to the pot, and let the veggies cook down for 5 to 7 minutes, until softened.

5. Pour in the stock, tomatoes, tomato puree, salt, pepper, spices, beans, and corn or hominy.

6. Taste the chili and adjust the spices to your liking. Add a tablespoon or two of the adobo sauce; this adds a little extra spice, so if the chili is already too spicy for you, go easy on it. Reduce the heat to low, cover, and simmer for at least 30 minutes.

INGREDIENTS (continued):

1 (15-ounce) can no-salt-added dark red kidney beans, drained and rinsed

2 (15-ounce) cans no-salt-added corn, drained and rinsed, or 1 (29-ounce) can hominy, drained and rinsed

For serving: sharp cheddar, fresh cilantro, and tortilla chips (all optional, but recommended)

INSTRUCTIONS (continued):

7. When you're ready to serve, mix in the cooked wheat berries.

8. Serve with cheese, chips, and cilantro.

NUTRITION INFORMATION PER SERVING:

Calories 302, Calories from Fat 65, Fat (g) 7.2, Saturated Fat (g) 1, Protein (g) 11.6, Carbohydrate (g) 50.2, Dietary Fiber (g) 14.1, Cholesterol (mg) 0, Sodium (mg) 755

CHAPTER THREE

PIZZA AND PASTA

WHOLE WHEAT FLAX PIZZA CRUST

SERVES 4 | MAKES ONE 12-INCH PIZZA CRUST

Homemade pizza is one of my favorite weeknight dinners. Pizzas are fun to make at home, and they can be healthy! This crust is a great base for hearty and healthy pizza at home. It's made with 100 percent whole wheat flour, flaxseed meal, olive oil, and just a little sugar to activate the yeast. Using instant yeast cuts down the rise time, and still gives you a fluffy, chewy crust.

INGREDIENTS:

2   teaspoons granulated sugar

⅔   cup warm water

1   package (2¼ teaspoons) quick-rise or instant yeast

1   teaspoon extra-virgin olive oil

1½ cups white whole wheat flour (or regular whole wheat flour), plus 1 tablespoon for kneading

1½ tablespoons ground flaxseed meal

½–1 teaspoon fine sea salt

INSTRUCTIONS:

1. Combine the sugar, water, and yeast in a bowl. Whisk until the yeast dissolves, and then let sit for 5 minutes. It should get very foamy in this time—if it doesn't, throw out what you have and start again (your yeast may be old, or your water may have been too hot).

2. After the yeast proofs, whisk in the olive oil. Add the flour, flaxseed meal, and salt. Use the paddle attachment of your mixer, or your hands and a wooden spoon, to bring the dough together.

3. Either switch your mixer attachment to the kneading hook, or transfer the dough to a floured surface and knead for 3 to 5 minutes. You may sprinkle in 1 tablespoon of additional flour as the machine kneads, or, if you're kneading with your hands, put ½ tablespoon of flour on your hands and ½ tablespoon on the surface you're using to knead. When it's finished, the dough will be smooth and elastic, and pop back when you poke it with your finger.

4. Place the dough in a lightly oiled bowl, flipping it around to evenly coat the dough. Cover loosely with plastic wrap and let it rise in a warm place for 1 hour.

5. When you're ready to bake, preheat the oven to 400°F. If you have a pizza stone, place it in the oven while it preheats.

6. Roll the dough into a 12-inch circle. Pinch the sides to form a crust, and then brush lightly with olive oil. Add desired toppings and bake for 17 to 25 minutes (baking times will vary depending on the type of toppings you use).

NUTRITION INFORMATION PER SERVING:
Calories 201, Calories from Fat 36, Fat (g) 4, Saturated Fat (g) 0.5, Protein (g) 7.6, Carbohydrate (g) 36.9, Dietary Fiber (g) 6.7, Cholesterol (mg) 0, Sodium (mg) 300

BBQ "CHICKEN" PIZZA

SERVES 4

I like putting a vegetarian twist on Ryan's favorite meals, and this BBQ "Chicken" Pizza is a prime example. Instead of chicken, this recipe uses seitan, also called "wheat meat," which is made up of wheat gluten. It has a much "meatier" texture than tofu, so it works well when you're trying to imitate the real thing. Since the recipe serves four, I intended to eat the leftovers for two workweek lunches, but Ryan devoured them before I had a chance—that's how I know I have a winner!

INGREDIENTS:

1   tablespoon olive oil, divided

8   ounces cubed seitan

6   tablespoons BBQ sauce, divided

1   recipe Whole Wheat Flax Pizza Crust (page 67)

¼   red onion, sliced

4   ounces fresh mozzarella, very thinly sliced

1   ounce goat cheese, crumbled (or substitute feta or blue cheese, if desired)

½   cup chopped cilantro

INSTRUCTIONS:

1. Preheat the oven to 400°F. If you have one, place a pizza stone in the oven while it preheats (this will help you get a crispier crust).

2. Heat ½ tablespoon of the olive oil in a nonstick skillet over medium heat. Add the seitan and cook, stirring frequently, for 5 minutes. It will begin to brown on the outside. Pour in 2 tablespoons of the BBQ sauce and cook for another 2 minutes, until the seitan soaks up the majority of the liquid. Remove from the heat.

3. Roll out the dough into a 12-inch circle. I like to do this on parchment paper so it doesn't stick to the surface. Brush on the remaining ½ tablespoon of olive oil, then brush on the remaining BBQ sauce, leaving about a ½-inch border. Top with the red onion, mozzarella slices, and BBQ seitan. Sprinkle with the crumbled goat cheese.

4. Transfer the crust to the preheated baking pan. Bake for 17 minutes, then broil for 2 to 3 minutes.

5. Top with chopped fresh cilantro.

NUTRITION INFORMATION PER SERVING:
Calories 454, Calories from Fat 149, Fat (g) 16.6, Saturated Fat (g) 4, Protein (g) 29.8, Carbohydrate (g) 50.7, Dietary Fiber (g) 7.8, Cholesterol (mg) 13, Sodium (mg) 881

The High-Protein Vegetarian Cookbook

GREEN MONSTER PIZZA WITH CRISPY KALE

SERVES 4

The term *green monster* often refers to bright green beverages, but this one is a super-flavorful pizza that supplies you with both protein and powerful superfood veggies. This recipe starts with a Basil-Spinach Pesto, which is topped with broccoli that gets nice and roasted in the oven. A bit of mozzarella brings some creaminess to the pizza, while crispy kale chips add great texture to every bite.

INGREDIENTS:

1   recipe Whole Wheat Flax Pizza Crust (page 67)

2½ cups broccoli florets

1   tablespoon olive oil, divided

5   ounces fresh mozzarella, thinly sliced

3   large lacinato kale leaves, large center stems removed, cut into 2-inch pieces

⅛   teaspoon fine sea salt

Basil-Spinach Pesto

2   tablespoons unsalted slivered raw almonds

2   cloves garlic

2   cups packed spinach leaves

1   cup packed fresh basil leaves

¼–½ teaspoon fine sea salt

1   tablespoon extra-virgin olive oil

INSTRUCTIONS:

1. Preheat the oven to 400°F. If you have one, place your pizza stone in the oven while it preheats.

2. To make the pesto, combine the almonds and garlic in a food processor. Pulse until chopped. Add the spinach, basil, and salt and process until finely chopped. Pour in the olive oil with the processor running, scraping down the sides as necessary.

3. Roll the pizza dough out into a 12-inch circle. Spoon on the pesto, leaving about a 1-inch border. Toss the broccoli florets with 1 teaspoon of the olive oil, then place them on top of the pesto. Place thin slices of mozzarella on top of the broccoli. Brush an additional teaspoon of olive oil on the outer crust of the pizza. Bake for 10 minutes.

4. While the pizza is cooking, toss the kale leaves with the remaining teaspoon of olive oil and ⅛ teaspoon salt. After the pizza has baked for 10 minutes, remove it from the oven and place the kale leaves on top. Bake for an additional 10 to 12 minutes, until the kale leaves are crispy.

NUTRITION INFORMATION PER SERVING:
Calories 394, Calories from Fat 185, Fat (g) 20.5, Saturated Fat (g) 4.1, Protein (g) 17.3, Carbohydrate (g) 42.3, Dietary Fiber (g) 9.5, Cholesterol (mg) 12, Sodium (mg) 586

ARTICHOKE AND LEMON RICOTTA CALZONES

SERVES 4

When I see artichokes on a menu, I have trouble giving my attention to anything else. When those artichokes are tucked inside a calzone? Done deal. This calzone starts with my Whole Wheat Flax Pizza Crust, which is filled with creamy lemon-thyme ricotta, juicy grape tomatoes, and those artichokes I love so much. I've eaten these with a side of marinara, but they're also delicious when eaten plain.

INGREDIENTS:

1 cup part-skim ricotta

¼ teaspoon fine sea salt, divided

1 clove garlic, minced

Juice of ¼ lemon

½ teaspoon grated lemon zest

1 teaspoon dried thyme

1 (14-ounce) can artichoke hearts, drained, rinsed, and roughly chopped

1 cup grape tomatoes, quartered

2 teaspoons olive oil

¼ teaspoon ground black pepper

1 recipe Whole Wheat Flax Pizza Crust (page 67)

¼ cup grated Parmesan cheese

1 egg, lightly beaten

INSTRUCTIONS:

1. Preheat the oven to 400°F. If you have one, place your pizza stone in the oven while it preheats.

2. Combine the ricotta, half the salt, garlic, lemon juice, lemon zest, and dried thyme in a bowl. Mix with a fork until incorporated.

3. In another bowl, stir together the artichokes, tomatoes, olive oil, remaining salt, and black pepper.

4. Divide the dough into four equal-sized balls.

5. Roll each ball of dough into an 8 x 6-inch oval on a piece of parchment.

6. Spread a quarter of the ricotta mixture on the bottom half of one oval, leaving a ½-inch border. Top with a quarter of the tomato-artichoke mixture, and then a quarter of the Parmesan. Fold the top half of the dough over the fillings and press the seam with your finger. Use the tines of a fork to seal the edges, then brush the calzone with egg wash. Make two slits in the top. Repeat with all the dough and fillings.

7. Bake the calzones for 15 to 20 minutes, until they're golden on top and cooked through on the bottom.

8. Eat plain, or serve with marinara.

NUTRITION INFORMATION PER SERVING:
Calories 388, Calories from Fat 124, Fat (g) 13.8, Saturated Fat (g) 5.1, Protein (g) 20.5, Carbohydrate (g) 49.2, Dietary Fiber (g) 10.3, Cholesterol (mg) 69, Sodium (mg) 717

CREAMY POTATO AND CARAMELIZED ONION PIZZA

SERVES 4

This pizza is based on one of my all-time favorite restaurant pizzas. It starts with a creamy Parmesan sauce, which is topped with thinly sliced potatoes, two types of cheese, rosemary, and black pepper, and then finished off with caramelized onions for a hint of sweetness.

INGREDIENTS:

Sauce

½ cup 1% cottage cheese

1 clove garlic

¼ cup grated Parmesan cheese

¼ teaspoon black pepper

Caramelized Onions

½ tablespoon olive oil

½ yellow onion, sliced

⅛ teaspoon salt

1 teaspoon dark brown sugar

¼ cup water (or as needed)

Pizza

1 recipe Whole Wheat Flax Pizza Crust (page 67)

½ medium-sized russet potato, peeled and thinly sliced

1 ounce Fontina cheese, shredded (about ¼ cup)

1 ounce Jarlsberg cheese, shredded (about ¼ cup)

¼ teaspoon black pepper

1 tablespoon fresh rosemary

½ tablespoon olive oil

INSTRUCTIONS:

Sauce

1. Combine all ingredients in a food processor and pulse until smooth. Set aside.

Onions

2. Heat the olive oil in a large skillet. Add the onion and cook for 10 minutes over medium-low heat, stirring occasionally.

3. After 10 minutes sprinkle in the salt and sugar. Continue to cook for another 30 to 35 minutes, stirring occasionally and adding more oil if the onions begin to stick. You can also add a bit of water if the onions look dry.

4. Once the onions are caramelized, remove them from the heat.

Pizza

5. Preheat the oven to 400°F.

6. Roll out the dough into a 12-inch circle. Spread on the sauce, then top with the potato, cheeses, black pepper, and rosemary. Drizzle with the olive oil.

7. Bake for 20 minutes, until all the cheese is melted and the crust is golden.

8. Top the hot pizza with the caramelized onions.

NUTRITION INFORMATION PER SERVING:
Calories 339, Calories from Fat 104, Fat (g) 11.5, Saturated Fat (g) 3.5, Protein (g) 16.9, Carbohydrate (g) 45.6, Dietary Fiber (g) 7.4, Cholesterol (mg) 14, Sodium (mg) 623

SPAGHETTI AND LENTIL-WALNUT "MEATBALLS"

SERVES 9

I have to admit that plain spaghetti with red sauce just doesn't do it for me. I need something hearty in there to fill me up and make me feel like I'm having a real meal. These vegetarian "meatballs" add savory texture to plain old spaghetti, plus they are made with protein-rich ingredients like lentils, navy beans, and whole wheat. I've served these to both meat-eaters and vegetarians, and they always receive rave reviews!

INGREDIENTS:

Lentil-Walnut "Meatballs"

2 slices whole wheat bread, toasted

½ cup black lentils, rinsed

1 cup water

1 (15-ounce) can navy beans, rinsed and drained

5 ounces sliced shiitake mushrooms

½ cup unsalted chopped raw walnuts

2 cloves garlic

1 teaspoon fine sea salt

¼ teaspoon onion powder

2 tablespoons grated Parmesan cheese

½ cup fresh basil, chopped

½ cup fresh parsley, chopped

1 large egg, lightly beaten

¼ cup whole wheat flour

16 ounces whole wheat spaghetti

INSTRUCTIONS:

Meatballs

1. Place the bread in a food processor and pulse until fine. Set aside.

2. Combine the lentils and water in a small saucepan. Bring to a light boil, then cover, reduce the heat to low, and allow to simmer for 25 minutes. Check the lentils frequently and add more water if needed. The lentils are ready when they are tender but not mushy.

3. Combine the lentils, beans, mushrooms, walnuts, garlic, salt, onion powder, Parmesan, basil, and parsley in a food processor. Pulse several times, scraping down the sides as necessary, until all the ingredients are very finely chopped. The beans will be mostly smooth, but the remaining ingredients should not be pureed. You may need to process the mixture in waves, depending on the size of your processor.

4. Stir the bread crumbs into the lentil-walnut mixture. Mix in the egg, and then sprinkle in the flour and stir until combined.

Spicy Basil Marinara

2 tablespoons olive oil

2 cloves garlic, minced

¼ cup chopped red onion

½ teaspoon fine sea salt

1 (28-ounce) can crushed tomatoes

½ teaspoon red pepper flakes

¼ cup fresh basil, chopped

5. Scoop 2 tablespoons of dough, shape into a ball, and place on a greased baking sheet. Repeat with remaining dough. Coat the "meatballs" with cooking spray—this will help them brown on top.

6. Bake for 35 to 40 minutes, until set and golden.

Sauce

7. While meatballs bake, heat the olive oil for the pasta sauce in a large saucepan over medium heat. Add the garlic and cook until fragrant, then add the onion and the salt. Stir for a few minutes, until the onion is translucent.

8. Add the tomatoes, red pepper flakes, and basil. Bring to a boil, then cover, reduce the heat to low, and let simmer for 20 minutes.

Assembly

9. Cook the pasta according to the package directions.

10. When all the elements are ready, combine the pasta with the sauce, and divide among nine bowls or plates. Top each serving with three meatballs.

NUTRITION INFORMATION PER SERVING:
Calories 393, Calories from Fat 88, Fat (g) 9.8, Saturated Fat (g) 1.4, Protein (g) 17.8, Carbohydrate (g) 62.6, Dietary Fiber (g) 13.4, Cholesterol (mg) 21, Sodium (mg) 511

CHICKPEA GNOCCHI WITH WHOLE-GRAIN MUSTARD CREAM SAUCE

SERVES 2

Gnocchi may sound intimidating to make, but if you follow the instructions below you can have tender, creamy homemade gnocchi in just 30 minutes. This recipe uses chickpeas (instead of potatoes) for the starchy base, which gives each dumpling a big boost in protein. The whole-grain mustard sauce is based on a meal I enjoyed immensely at a local restaurant. In this recipe, it's creamy, tangy, lightly textured, and goes wonderfully with the gnocchi.

INGREDIENTS:

Chickpea Gnocchi

1   (15-ounce) can chickpeas, rinsed and drained

2   tablespoons water

1   large egg yolk, lightly beaten

¼   cup white whole wheat flour (or regular whole wheat flour)

¼   teaspoon fine sea salt

¼   teaspoon freshly ground pepper

2   tablespoons grated Parmesan

Mustard Cream Sauce

½   tablespoon unsalted butter

½   tablespoon all-purpose flour

½   cup 2% milk

⅛   teaspoon salt

¼   teaspoon pepper

Small pinch of ground nutmeg

2   tablespoons whole-grain mustard

INSTRUCTIONS:

Gnocchi

1. Puree the beans in a food processor with the water until smooth. Transfer to a bowl.

2. Add the beaten egg yolk, and then use a fork to mix in the flour, salt, pepper, and Parmesan.

3. Knead the mixture for 3 to 5 minutes on a lightly floured surface, until it's smooth. You will need an additional 3 to 4 tablespoons of flour for your hands and the surface during this process, to keep it from sticking. It is ready when it comes together into a smooth dough.

4. Divide the dough into four equal-sized balls.

5. Roll each ball into a strand about 10 inches long.

6. Cut each strand into ½-inch pieces.

7. Roll each piece of dough on the back of a fork, so that one side is imprinted with the fork tines, and the other with an imprint of your finger. This will create more crevices for sauce to sink into.

8. Drop the gnocchi dough into boiling water in waves, being careful not to overcrowd the pot. When they float to the top (after just a couple of minutes), use a slotted spoon to remove them and set them aside in a single layer (otherwise they may stick together).

Sauce

9. Melt the butter over medium heat in a saucepan. Add the flour and whisk until it forms a paste. Add the milk, salt, pepper, and nutmeg, and whisk frequently until thickened (about 5 to 7 minutes). Remove from the heat and whisk in the whole-grain mustard. Taste and adjust the salt/pepper level to your liking.

10. Put the gnocchi in a large bowl, and slowly pour in the sauce. Divide into two bowls, and top with a sprinkle of Parmesan (if desired).

NUTRITION INFORMATION PER SERVING:
Calories 405, Calories from Fat 108, Fat (g) 12, Saturated Fat (g) 4.6, Protein (g) 20.2, Carbohydrate (g) 56.8, Dietary Fiber (g) 12.9, Cholesterol (mg) 106, Sodium (mg) 922

THAI PEANUT SOBA NOODLES

SERVES 5

Save money by making your own Thai-inspired dish at home! The mix of peanut butter, brown sugar, soy sauce, and colorful veggies helps these noodles find that perfect balance between salty and sweet. Feel free to swap the veggies in this dish for your favorites; broccoli, bok choy, and water chestnuts would all be fabulous. Be creative and make it your own!

INGREDIENTS:

Peanut Buckwheat Soy Noodles

1   (8.8-ounce) bag buckwheat soba noodles (or a mix of buckwheat and wheat)

2   tablespoons peanut oil

1   clove garlic, minced

1   bunch green onions, sliced up to where the leaves part

1   large carrot, shredded (about 1¾ cups)

1   red bell pepper, chopped

¾   cup shelled cooked edamame

5   tablespoons unsalted crushed peanuts

Peanut Sauce

1   cup light coconut milk

1   tablespoon Thai red curry paste

2   tablespoons soy sauce

¼   cup creamy peanut butter

2   tablespoons packed dark brown sugar

⅛   teaspoon kosher salt

½   teaspoon freshly grated gingerroot

⅛–¼ teaspoon cayenne pepper (optional)

½   tablespoon apple cider vinegar

¼   cup water

INSTRUCTIONS:

1. Cook the noodles according to the package directions.

Sauce

2. While the noodles cook, combine all of the peanut sauce ingredients in a saucepan over medium-low heat, whisking constantly. Bring to a low boil, and continue to whisk for 3 to 5 minutes. Remove from the heat and set aside (it will thicken slightly as it cools).

Noodles

3. Heat the oil in a large skillet over medium heat. Add the garlic and cook for 30 seconds, until fragrant. Stir in the onions and cook for 2 to 3 minutes, until slightly softened. Add the carrot, red bell pepper, and edamame, and cook for 3 to 5 minutes. The red bell pepper and the carrots will be slightly softened but still have a bit of a bite.

4. Drain the noodles, then transfer to a large bowl. Pour in the vegetables and peanut sauce, stirring until the sauce is well distributed.

5. Separate into five bowls, and top each bowl with 1 tablespoon of crushed peanuts.

NUTRITION INFORMATION PER SERVING:

Calories 389, Calories from Fat 157, Fat (g) 17.5, Saturated Fat (g) 3.7, Protein (g) 13.7, Carbohydrate (g) 49.5, Dietary Fiber (g) 6, Cholesterol (mg) 0, Sodium (mg) 774

PASTA E FAGIOLI

SERVES 5

Pasta e Fagioli, a.k.a. pasta and beans, is simple Italian comfort food at its finest. This meal can be in your bowl in 30 minutes, but it tastes like it simmered for hours. It walks the line between a soup and pasta, with a thick, rich tomato base filled with rosemary, basil, oregano, and thyme. After the flavors deepen in the simmering process, you puree a portion of the soup to give it a partially smooth texture. If you don't have macaroni on hand, any small pasta will do.

INGREDIENTS:

- 2   tablespoons unsalted butter
- 1   clove garlic, minced
- ½   small yellow onion, diced
- 1   (28-ounce) can no-salt-added whole peeled tomatoes
- 1   (15-ounce) can cannellini beans, rinsed and drained
- 1   (15-ounce) can red kidney beans, rinsed and drained
- ¼   cup sun-dried tomatoes, chopped
- 2   tablespoons tomato paste
- ¾   teaspoon fine sea salt
- ¼   teaspoon ground black pepper
- 1   teaspoon dried thyme
- 1   teaspoon dried oregano
- 1   teaspoon dried basil
- 1   teaspoon dried rosemary
- 2   bay leaves
- 1   cup whole wheat elbow macaroni

INSTRUCTIONS:

1. Melt the butter in a large saucepan over medium heat. Add the garlic and cook for 30 seconds, then add the onion. Cook the onion until softened, about 3 minutes.

2. Pour in the tomatoes and use a large spoon to break them apart a bit. Add the beans, sun-dried tomatoes, tomato paste, salt, pepper, all herbs, and bay leaves. Simmer for 20 minutes.

3. Cook the macaroni according to the package directions.

4. After the bean mixture is done simmering, remove the bay leaves, transfer 3 cups to a food processor, and puree until smooth. Pour the pureed mixture back into the saucepan, then add the cooked macaroni.

NUTRITION INFORMATION PER SERVING:
Calories 297, Calories from Fat 51, Fat (g) 5.7, Saturated Fat (g) 3.1, Protein (g) 14.8, Carbohydrate (g) 50.8, Dietary Fiber (g) 11.7, Cholesterol (mg) 12, Sodium (mg) 554

PEA PESTO ORECHIETTE

SERVES 4

This very green pasta is full of flavor and protein! This recipe takes standard basil pesto to the next level of flavor with the addition of sautéed green peas, shallots, and a touch of lemon. Green peas not only add protein to the dish, but also give a richness to the sauce that works well with the nutty toasted almonds. This pasta is vegan-friendly, but if you're not vegan I highly recommend topping it with a sprinkle of grated Parmesan.

INGREDIENTS:

8   ounces whole wheat orechiette (other shell-shaped pasta will work as well)

3   tablespoons olive oil

2   cloves garlic, minced

1   shallot, diced

½   teaspoon fine sea salt, divided

1½ cups frozen green peas

¼   cup vegetable broth

¼   cup unsalted slivered raw almonds

½   cup fresh basil

Juice of 1 lemon

¼   teaspoon ground white pepper

¼   teaspoon ground black pepper

Grated Parmesan cheese (optional, for topping)

INSTRUCTIONS:

1. Cook the pasta according to the package directions.

2. Heat the olive oil in a large skillet over medium heat. Add the garlic and cook for 30 seconds, and then add the shallot and half of the salt. Cook for 3 to 4 minutes, until soft.

3. Pour in the peas, remaining salt, and broth. Simmer for 5 minutes, until the peas are soft and have soaked up some of the broth.

4. While the peas are cooking, toast the slivered almonds in the oven at 350°F for about 7 to 12 minutes, until golden.

5. Combine the almonds and basil in a food processor. Pulse until very finely chopped. Add the lemon, white pepper, black pepper, peas, and sauce to the food processor and process until smooth.

6. Toss the pasta with the pea pesto, and top with Parmesan (if desired).

NUTRITION INFORMATION PER SERVING:
Calories 381, Calories from Fat 137, Fat (g) 15.2, Saturated Fat (g) 1.7, Protein (g) 12.4, Carbohydrate (g) 51, Dietary Fiber (g) 9, Cholesterol (mg) 0, Sodium (mg) 390

LINGUINE WITH CREAMY TOMATO VODKA SAUCE

SERVES 8

Although I like simple marinara sauces, sometimes I get a craving for something thick and creamy. Traditional tomato vodka sauces get their creamy look and texture from heavy cream. This version is every bit as comforting and decadent tasting, but gets its creaminess from pureed chickpeas and just ¼ cup of half-and-half. Ryan, who loves ordering vodka sauce at restaurants, raved about this version, and even ate two servings in one sitting—from a man who usually eats less than me, that's a good sign!

INGREDIENTS:

2   tablespoons olive oil

3   cloves garlic, minced

½   medium-sized yellow onion, diced

¾   teaspoon fine sea salt (or to taste), divided

1   (28-ounce) can crushed tomatoes with basil

1   (15-ounce) can chickpeas, drained and rinsed

1   teaspoon dried oregano

1   teaspoon dried basil

2   tablespoons tomato paste

1   tablespoon packed dark brown sugar

1   pound whole wheat linguine

¼   cup half-and-half or whole milk

5   tablespoons vodka

½   cup grated Parmesan cheese

INSTRUCTIONS:

1. Heat the olive oil in a large pot over medium heat. Add the garlic and cook for 30 seconds, then add the onion and half of the salt. Cook for a few minutes, until the onion is soft.

2. Pour in the tomatoes, chickpeas, oregano, basil, tomato paste, sugar, and remaining salt. Bring to a boil, then reduce to a simmer for 15 minutes, stirring occasionally.

3. While the sauce simmers, get the water for your pasta ready. Cook the pasta according to the package directions.

4. Transfer the sauce to a food processor or blender and process until smooth. Pour back into the pot and stir in the half-and-half and vodka. Bring to a boil, then reduce to a simmer for another 5 minutes. Pour in the cooked pasta, and toss for 1 minute.

5. Divide the cooked pasta among eight plates. Top each plate with 1 tablespoon of grated Parmesan.

NUTRITION INFORMATION PER SERVING:
Calories 380, Calories from Fat 70, Fat (g) 7.8, Saturated Fat (g) 1.8, Protein (g) 12.7, Carbohydrate (g) 58.1, Dietary Fiber (g) 10.6, Cholesterol (mg) 6, Sodium (mg) 310

WHITE CHEDDAR MAC AND CHEESE

SERVES 8

I'm not proud of it, but I have to admit that every so often I just get a craving for white cheddar mac and cheese from the box. This recipe provides a healthy alternative to the box, with a super-creamy and flavorful sauce made with a touch of butter, reduced-fat milk, sharp white cheddar, and . . . cauliflower! The cauliflower helps thicken the sauce, and adds extra protein to the dish. This recipe serves eight, but if you're not going to go through it all in one night, don't worry—add a splash of milk before reheating in the microwave and you can enjoy this healthy comfort food for days.

INGREDIENTS:

1   head cauliflower, chopped

2   tablespoons olive oil, divided

1   tablespoon unsalted butter

1   tablespoon unbleached all-purpose flour

2   cups 2% milk

¼   teaspoon ground pepper

⅛   teaspoon freshly grated nutmeg

¼   teaspoon onion powder

1   teaspoon fine sea salt, divided

4   ounces sharp white cheddar, shredded (about 1 cup)

16 ounces whole wheat macaroni

2   cloves garlic, minced

1   (10.5-ounce) container cherry tomatoes, halved

3   cups packed baby spinach, chopped

INSTRUCTIONS:

1. Bring a large pot of water to a boil. Add the cauliflower and cook until it easily falls apart, about 10 minutes. Use a slotted spoon to transfer it to a blender or food processor. Add 1 cup of the water you cooked the cauliflower in, and puree until smooth. Add 1 tablespoon of the olive oil as the processor is running.

2. Melt the butter in a medium-sized saucepan over medium-low heat. Add the flour and whisk until it becomes a paste and smells somewhat nutty. Pour in the milk, pepper, nutmeg, onion powder, and half of the salt. Increase the heat to medium, bring the mixture to a light boil, and then reduce the heat to medium-low again. Stir constantly for 5 to 7 minutes until the sauce thickens. Remove from the heat and stir in the cheese until it melts, then mix in the pureed cauliflower.

3. Cook the pasta according to the package directions.

The High-Protein Vegetarian Cookbook

4. Heat the remaining 1 tablespoon olive oil in a large skillet. Add the garlic and cook until fragrant. Pour in the cherry tomatoes and the remaining salt, and cook until softened, about 5 minutes. Add the spinach and cook until it wilts, about 30 seconds.

5. Add the cooked pasta and cheese sauce to the pan with the vegetables. Stir until combined.

6. Divide the pasta among eight plates or bowls.

NUTRITION INFORMATION PER SERVING:
Calories 364, Calories from Fat 107, Fat (g) 11.9, Saturated Fat (g) 5.4, Protein (g) 16.4, Carbohydrate (g) 53, Dietary Fiber (g) 7.3, Cholesterol (mg) 24, Sodium (mg) 458

CHAPTER FOUR

BURGERS AND SANDWICHES

SPICY THAI PEANUT VEGGIE BURGERS

SERVES 6

Although I grab Thai takeout every so often, sometimes I need a quick meal that gives me all the flavor I crave, while allowing me to save some money and stay comfy at home. These burgers come together easily, are packed with the flavors of my favorite Thai takeout, and include healthy, fresh ingredients.

INGREDIENTS:

1 (15-ounce) can no-salt-added chickpeas, rinsed, drained, and patted dry

2 tablespoons Thai red curry paste

1 clove garlic

¼ cup plus 2 tablespoons creamy no-sugar-added peanut butter

1 tablespoon honey

½ teaspoon kosher salt

¼ teaspoon ground ginger

1½ teaspoons hot sauce (such as sriracha)

1½ teaspoons soy sauce

¼ cup cilantro, chopped

½ cup shredded carrot

¼ cup finely chopped red onion

¼ cup roasted peanuts, finely chopped

½ red bell pepper, finely chopped

1 large egg

¼ cup whole wheat flour

6 whole wheat burger buns

INSTRUCTIONS:

1. Preheat the oven to 350°F.

2. Combine the chickpeas, red curry paste, garlic, peanut butter, honey, salt, ginger, hot sauce, and soy sauce in a food processor. Pulse until the mixture is mostly smooth. Transfer to a large bowl and stir in the cilantro, carrot, red onion, peanuts, and red bell pepper. Add the egg and stir until it's fully incorporated. Stir in the flour.

3. Shape the dough into six patties and place them on a parchment-lined baking sheet. The mixture will be very sticky, so you may need to wipe off your hands after you form each patty. Coat the top of the patties with cooking spray.

4. Bake for 15 minutes. Remove from the oven, flip, coat again with cooking spray, and bake for another 15 minutes.

Lime Soy Slaw

2 cups chopped savoy cabbage

Juice of ½ lime (1 tablespoon)

1 teaspoon soy sauce

1 teaspoon peanut oil

⅛ teaspoon kosher salt

⅛ teaspoon black pepper

½ teaspoon garlic powder

½ teaspoon honey

5. While the patties bake, mix together all of the slaw ingredients in a large bowl.

6. Place each patty on a toasted whole wheat bun, then top with the slaw. Red pepper slices and cilantro are great add-ons as well.

NUTRITION INFORMATION PER SERVING:

Calories 358, Calories from Fat 121, Fat (g) 13.5, Saturated Fat (g) 2.4, Protein (g) 14, Carbohydrate (g) 47.8, Dietary Fiber (g) 9.4, Cholesterol (mg) 31, Sodium (mg) 743

PROTEIN POWERHOUSE VEGGIE BURGERS

SERVES 11

These burgers are full of so many superfoods, I couldn't even fit any in the title of the recipe: black beans, beluga (black) lentils, quinoa, oats, flax, and walnuts. Each patty is hearty, rich, spicy, and downright irresistible when slathered in a smooth roasted red pepper Greek yogurt sauce. I love these burgers as written below, but they're also great when crumbled on top of salads for extra protein with your greens.

INGREDIENTS:

Protein Powerhouse Patty

4 cups water

1 cup beluga lentils, picked through and rinsed

½ cup warm water mixed with 3 tablespoons flaxseed meal

2 (15-ounce) cans no-salt-added black beans, drained, rinsed, and patted dry

1 cup cooked quinoa

½ cup oats, processed into flour (gluten-free if desired)

3 cloves garlic, minced

½ red onion, diced

1 red pepper, finely chopped

½ cup walnuts, chopped

1 tablespoon ground cumin

½ teaspoon cayenne

1 teaspoon sriracha (or other hot sauce)

1 teaspoon kosher salt

¼ teaspoon freshly ground black pepper

11 whole wheat burger buns

INSTRUCTIONS:

1. Bring 4 cups of water to a boil. Do not add any salt.

2. Add the beluga lentils to the boiling water, let cook for 5 minutes, and then reduce the heat to a simmer for 10 to 15 minutes. When the lentils are tender, drain the excess water and rinse the lentils until the water runs clear. Pat dry with a paper towel and set aside.

3. Combine the ground flax with the warm water and let sit for 10 minutes.

4. Puree the lentils with 1 can of the black beans. Pour into a large bowl with the remaining black beans, quinoa, oat flour, garlic, red onion, red pepper, walnuts, flax-water mixture, and spices. Taste the mixture and adjust the spices to your liking.

5. Refrigerate the mixture for 1 hour. This isn't necessary, but will make your life a lot easier as you form the patties.

6. Preheat the oven to 375°F.

Roasted Red Pepper Crema

1 (10-ounce) jar roasted red peppers, drained

¼ cup sour cream

½ cup 2% plain Greek yogurt

½ teaspoon kosher salt

¼ teaspoon cayenne

1 tablespoon olive oil

NUTRITION INFORMATION PER SERVING:
Calories 369, Calories from Fat 92, Fat (g) 10.3, Saturated Fat (g) 1.9, Protein (g) 16.6, Carbohydrate (g) 55.9, Dietary Fiber (g) 12.5, Cholesterol (mg) 4, Sodium (mg) 499

7. To form the patties, grab a handful of the patty mixture and form it into a ball. It will be a bit sticky. Drop it onto a parchment-lined sheet and press down lightly with your fingers to flatten. Repeat with the remaining mixture to form a total of 11 patties. Bake for 12 minutes on one side, flip carefully with a spatula, and bake on the other side for another 12 minutes.

8. While the patties are baking, combine the red peppers, sour cream, Greek yogurt, salt, and cayenne in a food processor. Pulse until smooth, then pour in the oil with the processor running. Set aside until the burgers are ready.

9. Serve each patty on a whole wheat bun with Roasted Red Pepper Crema and any other desired toppings.

WILD RICE, MUSHROOM, AND NAVY BEAN BURGERS

SERVES 5

A flavorful, texture-filled vegetarian patty made with wild rice, mushrooms, and navy beans. These patties are easy to make and hearty enough to win over even the most stubborn meat-eaters. Perfect when served on a toasted whole wheat bun with a slice of juicy tomato and melted cheese.

INGREDIENTS

½   cup dry, uncooked wild rice

1½ cups water

2   slices whole wheat bread (enough to make roughly 2 cups bread crumbs)

3   tablespoons olive oil

3   cloves garlic, minced

½   cup diced red onion

4   ounces sliced white mushrooms,

1   (15-ounce) can cooked navy beans

½   teaspoon kosher salt

⅛   teaspoon cayenne

½   teaspoon yellow mustard powder

1   tablespoon dried oregano

½   teaspoon chili powder

1   egg

5   whole wheat burger buns

NUTRITION INFORMATION PER SERVING:
Calories 372, Calories from Fat 110, Fat (g) 12.2, Saturated Fat (g) 2, Protein (g) 13.9, Carbohydrate (g) 55, Dietary Fiber (g) 11, Cholesterol (mg) 37, Sodium (mg) 533

INSTRUCTIONS:

1. First, cook the wild rice: Bring the water to a boil, and add the rice. Cover, turn the heat down to low, and cook for 45 to 50 minutes.

2. Preheat the oven to 400°F.

3. Pulse the bread in a food processor until the slices become coarse crumbs.

4. Heat the olive oil in a skillet over medium heat. Add the garlic and cook for 30 seconds. Pour in the onion and cook until translucent. Add the bread crumbs and cook, stirring frequently, for 2 to 3 minutes, until lightly browned.

5. Place the mushrooms in a food processor and pulse until they are finely chopped. Set aside.

6. Place the navy beans in the food processor and pulse until mostly smooth.

7. In a large bowl, combine the wild rice, mushrooms, bread crumb mixture, salt, and spices. Taste and adjust the spice level to your liking. Add the egg and mix until well incorporated.

8. Form five patties, and place on a baking sheet lined with parchment paper.

9. Bake for 25 minutes, flipping halfway through.

10. Serve on a toasted bun with your favorite toppings.

DOUBLE BEAN JUICY LUCY BURGERS

Cheese-stuffed burgers (aka "Juicy Lucys") originated in my home state of Minnesota, and I've observed several friendly arguments about which local bar makes the best version. As a cheese lover, I've always been a bit jealous of these burgers, so I decided to make my own version. This patty has great texture from oats and pepitas that are mixed in with the spiced beans, but the main point, of course, is that the outside leads to a melty, sharp cheddar center.

INGREDIENTS:

- 2 tablespoons ground flaxseed mixed with 6 tablespoons warm water
- 1 (15-ounce) can no-salt-added black beans, rinsed, drained, and patted dry
- 1 (15-ounce) can no-salt-added red kidney beans, rinsed, drained, and patted dry
- 1 tablespoon low-sodium soy sauce
- 2 cloves garlic, minced
- 1 shallot, diced
- ½ cup old-fashioned oats
- ½ cup unsalted hulled raw pepitas
- ½ teaspoon dried oregano
- ½ teaspoon paprika
- ½ teaspoon chili powder
- ¼ teaspoon ground cumin
- 3 tablespoons cilantro, chopped
- ½ teaspoon ground black pepper
- ½ teaspoon fine sea salt, or to taste
- 1 tablespoon olive oil
- 2½ ounces sharp cheddar, cubed
- 5 whole wheat hamburger buns

INSTRUCTIONS:

1. Combine the flaxseed and water, mix with a fork, and let sit for 5 minutes.

2. Pour the beans in a bowl and mash well with a fork. Mix in the soy sauce, garlic, shallot, oats, pepitas, all spices, and olive oil. Taste and adjust the seasonings to your liking.

3. Pour in the flax mixture, mix well, and refrigerate for 30 minutes.

4. Preheat the oven to 350°F.

5. Scoop out ¼ cup of burger mixture, and flatten into a patty. Top with ½ ounce of cheddar, and then shape another patty out of ¼ cup of the mixture to place on top. Make sure to seal the sides completely, and pack the patty together tightly so no cheese melts out while the burgers bake. Repeat with remaining bean mixture and cheese. This recipe will make five large patties.

6. Place the patties on a parchment-lined baking sheet, and bake for 15 to 20 minutes on each side. Let sit for 5 minutes before serving.

7. Serve each burger on a whole wheat bun with desired toppings.

NUTRITION INFORMATION PER SERVING:
Calories 457, Calories from Fat 157, Fat (g) 17.5, Saturated Fat (g) 5, Protein (g) 22, Carbohydrate (g) 57.5, Dietary Fiber (g) 12.9, Cholesterol (mg) 15, Sodium (mg) 617

FAUX SLOPPY JOES

SERVES 8

Even as a non-meat-eater, I can appreciate the layers of flavor in sloppy joes: sweet, salty, tangy . . . a whole mess of tasty. Green lentils and chopped seitan (a.k.a. "wheat meat") replace the ground beef in this version, and serve as a perfect base to soak up the flavors of the rich sloppy joe sauce. Serve each sloppy joe with crunchy kettle chips to scoop up all that delicious sloppiness.

INGREDIENTS:

1   cup green lentils, rinsed and picked through

3   cups water

8   ounces cubed seitan

1½ tablespoons olive oil

3   cloves garlic, minced

½   red onion, diced

¼–½ teaspoon fine sea salt

1   green pepper, diced

1   large carrot, peeled and diced

1   cup tomato sauce

¼   cup ketchup

3   tablespoons packed dark brown sugar

2   tablespoons tomato paste

2   tablespoons Dijon mustard

¼   teaspoon ground black pepper

1   teaspoon ground white pepper

½   teaspoon onion powder

1   tablespoon chili powder

2   tablespoons vegan Worcestershire sauce (optional)

8   whole wheat burger buns

INSTRUCTIONS:

1. Bring the lentils and water to a boil in a medium-sized saucepan. Reduce the heat to low, cover, and let simmer for 20 to 30 minutes, until the lentils are tender but not mushy. Drain any excess water and set aside.

2. Place the seitan in a food processor and pulse a few times, until you have seitan crumbles. Set aside.

3. Heat the olive oil in a large fry pan. Stir the garlic into the olive oil and cook until fragrant. Add the onion and salt, and cook for 2 to 3 minutes, until softened. Pour in the pepper, carrot, and crumbled seitan, and cook for 7 to 10 minutes, until the veggies are softened.

4. Add the lentils, along with all remaining ingredients, and cook on medium-low for 10 to 15 minutes, stirring frequently, until thickened.

5. Top each bun with ½ cup of filling.

NUTRITION INFORMATION PER SERVING:
Calories 320, Calories from Fat 54, Fat (g) 6, Saturated Fat (g) 0.8, Protein (g) 19, Carbohydrate (g) 51.4, Dietary Fiber (g) 10.7, Cholesterol (mg) 0, Sodium (mg) 792

The High-Protein Vegetarian Cookbook

OPEN-FACED PISTACHIO TOFU SANDWICH

SERVES 6

Sandwiches are a great go-to weeknight meal, but I like to switch things up to keep boredom at bay. This sandwich is full of texture and flavor, with crispy pistachio-crusted baked tofu, creamy mozzarella, and Sun-Dried Tomato and Basil Spread. If you're not in the mood for a sandwich, the pistachio tofu can be eaten alone with a side of marinara, or cut up and added to salads.

INGREDIENTS:

1   (14-ounce) container extra-firm tofu

½   cup unsalted roasted pistachio halves

1   teaspoon dried rosemary

½   cup panko bread crumbs

½   teaspoon fine sea salt

¼   teaspoon garlic powder

½   cup unbleached all-purpose flour

2   egg whites

½   cup low-fat buttermilk

1   tablespoon Dijon mustard

2   tablespoons coconut oil, divided

6   slices artisan whole wheat bread

1   medium tomato, thinly sliced

3   ounces fresh mozzarella, thinly sliced

Fresh basil, for serving

NUTRITION INFORMATION PER SERVING:
Calories 382, Calories from Fat 184, Fat (g) 20.4, Saturated Fat (g) 6.6, Protein (g) 20.4, Carbohydrate (g) 33.5, Dietary Fiber (g) 4.9, Cholesterol (mg) 6, Sodium (mg) 533

INSTRUCTIONS:

1. Preheat the oven to 375°F.

2. Cut the tofu into six slices. Place the slices on a kitchen towel, then top with another towel. Top with something heavy (a cast-iron pot, textbooks, or the like) and set aside for 10 to 15 minutes.

3. Process the pistachios and rosemary in a food processor until the nuts are finely chopped. Add to a bowl with the bread crumbs, salt, and garlic powder.

4. Set up three bowls: one with the flour, another with the egg whites, buttermilk, and Dijon mustard whisked together, and the third with the bread crumb mixture.

5. Dip each piece of tofu first in the flour, then in the egg-buttermilk, and finally in the bread crumbs. Make sure you coat the tofu on all sides with each ingredient. Place the dipped slices on a greased or parchment-lined baking sheet.

6. Bake the coated tofu slices for 35 to 40 minutes.

7. While the tofu bakes, combine the sun-dried tomatoes, basil, garlic, and salt in a food processor. Pour in a tablespoon of the water that you soaked the sun-dried tomatoes in. Pulse until very finely chopped. Add the olive oil while the processor is running.

Sun-Dried Tomato and Basil Spread

½ cup sun-dried tomato halves, soaked in warm water for 5 minutes

½ cup loosely packed basil leaves

2 cloves garlic

¼ teaspoon fine sea salt

1 tablespoon water (from the soaked sun-dried tomatoes)

1 tablespoon olive oil

8. Melt half of the coconut oil in a large nonstick fry pan over medium heat. Place the baked tofu slices on the heated pan, and cook for 2 minutes, until golden and crispy. Flip the slices and melt the remaining coconut oil. Cook for another 2 minutes.

9. Spread the Sun-Dried Tomato and Basil Spread onto each piece of bread. Top with a slice of baked tofu, a tomato slice, and a thin slice of mozzarella. Broil in the oven for 5 minutes, until the bread crust is toasted and the mozzarella is melted.

10. Top with fresh basil. Eat with a fork and knife.

LENTIL AND WALNUT TACOS

SERVES 4

Taco night works well for large groups, because everyone can fill their tortillas with whatever they want. Even when it's just the two of us, Ryan and I like making tacos because we have different ideas of what they should be filled with; I like to keep it simple with tomatoes, cilantro, and a tiny dab of sour cream, whereas he likes to fill his to the brim with cheese, hot sauce, lettuce, and a huge spoonful of sour cream. We can, however, agree on this super-healthy vegetarian taco filling. Made with French green lentils, walnuts, and spices, it gives tacos tons of flavor, texture, and protein, while still being versatile enough to work with a variety of taco toppings.

INGREDIENTS:

- 1   cup French green lentils, picked through and rinsed
- 3   cups water
- ½   cup unsalted walnut pieces
- 1   tablespoon olive oil
- 2   cloves garlic
- ½   red onion, chopped
- ¾   teaspoon fine sea salt, or to taste
- 1   tablespoon tomato paste
- ¼   cup no-salt-added tomato sauce
- ¾   teaspoon chili powder
- ⅛   teaspoon crushed red pepper flakes
- ½   teaspoon dried oregano
- ½   teaspoon paprika
- ¾   teaspoon ground cumin
- ½   teaspoon freshly ground pepper
- 8   corn tortillas

INSTRUCTIONS:

1. Combine the lentils with the water in a medium-sized sauce pan. Bring to a boil, then reduce to a simmer for 20 to 30 minutes, until the lentils are tender but not mushy. Do *not* add any salt to the water. When the lentils are cooked, drain any excess water.

2. While the lentils cook, toast the walnuts by placing them in an oven for 5 to 7 minutes at 325°F, shaking once so they cook evenly.

3. Place the cooked lentils and toasted walnuts in a food processor. Pulse a few times, until the walnuts and lentils are just roughly chopped (do not over-process). If you have a small processor, do this in waves; otherwise the lentils at the bottom will puree and the ingredients at the top won't get chopped.

4. Heat the oil in a large saucepan over medium heat. Add the garlic and cook for 30 seconds, then add the onion and salt. Cook for a few minutes, until the onion is soft. Add the lentil and walnut mixture, along with the tomato paste, tomato sauce, and remaining spices. Stir until the spices are incorporated and the mixture is warmed throughout.

5. Divide the tortillas between two damp towels (four tortillas each). Wrap the towels around the tortillas, and microwave for 20 to 30 seconds.

6. Distribute the filling among the eight warm tortillas, and add your desired toppings: sour cream, cilantro, salsa, avocado, cheese, what have you.

NUTRITION INFORMATION PER SERVING:
Calories 408, Calories from Fat 138, Fat (g) 15.3, Saturated Fat (g) 1.7, Protein (g) 17.6, Carbohydrate (g) 55.4, Dietary Fiber (g) 15.6, Cholesterol (mg) 0, Sodium (mg) 515

Burgers and Sandwiches

CHILI-ROASTED SWEET POTATO AND BLACK BEAN TACOS WITH CILANTRO LIME CREAM

SERVES 3

Some people like their sweet potatoes covered in butter and sugar, but I love the sweet spuds with a little bit of spice. These tacos combine chili-roasted sweet potatoes with protein-rich black beans.

INGREDIENTS:

Chili-Roasted Sweet Potato and Black Bean Tacos

1 medium-sized sweet potato, peeled and cut into ½-inch cubes

2 tablespoons olive oil, divided

½ teaspoon fine sea salt, or to taste, divided

1½ teaspoons chili powder

¼ teaspoon ground cayenne

1 teaspoon ground cumin

1 (15-ounce) can no-salt-added black beans, rinsed and drained

½ cup cilantro, chopped

6 small corn tortillas

6 tablespoons sour cream

Cilantro Lime Cream

⅔ cup cilantro

2 cloves garlic

½ cup 2% plain Greek yogurt

¼ cup sour cream

¼ teaspoon fine sea salt

⅛ teaspoon ground pepper

Juice of ½ lime

1 tablespoon olive oil

INSTRUCTIONS:

1. Preheat the oven to 375°F.

2. In a large bowl, toss the cubed sweet potato with 1½ tablespoons of the olive oil, half the salt, chili powder, cayenne, and cumin. Roast in the oven for 10 to 12 minutes, until tender.

3. While the potato is baking, combine the black beans, remaining salt, remaining olive oil, and cilantro in the same bowl you used for the sweet potatoes. There will be some leftover spices on the sides that you can incorporate into the beans as you stir.

4. When the potato is cooked, add it to the beans.

5. To make the cream sauce, pulse together the cilantro and garlic in a food processor until finely chopped. Add the Greek yogurt, sour cream, salt, pepper, and lime, then process until smooth. Add the olive oil while the processor is running.

6. Place the tortillas between two damp towels and microwave for 20 to 30 seconds. Top the tortillas with the Cilantro Lime Cream, the bean-potato mixture, and a dollop of sour cream.

NUTRITION INFORMATION PER SERVING (2 TACOS):
Calories 404, Calories from Fat 143, Fat (g) 15.9, Saturated Fat (g) 5, Protein (g) 12.1, Carbohydrate (g) 53.4, Dietary Fiber (g) 9.6, Cholesterol (mg) 19, Sodium (mg) 461

NUTRITION INFORMATION PER SERVING (⅓ OF CILANTRO LIME CREAM):
Calories 116, Calories from Fat 77, Fat (g) 8.5, Saturated Fat (g) 3.3, Protein (g) 4.7, Carbohydrate (g) 4, Dietary Fiber (g) 0.2, Cholesterol (mg) 15, Sodium (mg) 226

BAKED QUINOA FALAFEL PITA WITH TZATZIKI

SERVES 4

College taught me many things, but in the food department I'm thankful that my college cafeteria introduced me to falafels. When I walked up to the vegetarian-friendly line my freshman year, I had never heard of the little fried chickpea balls, but the obsession started immediately after I bit into my first one. It took me a while to perfect a recipe to use at home, but I've found that the spice mixture below brings me back to that college cafeteria experience. I like adding quinoa to my falafels because it adds extra fiber and protein, as well as a boost in texture. Instead of deep-frying my falafels, I simply bake them to firm them up, then quickly pan-fry them to give them a good crunch on the outside. The refreshing tzatziki is tangy, cool, and a perfect balance to the spiced falafel patties.

INGREDIENTS:

Quinoa Falafels

½ cup water

¼ cup quinoa, uncooked

1 (14.5-ounce) can chickpeas, drained, rinsed, and patted dry

¼ cup chopped red onion

2 cloves garlic

½ cup flat-leaf parsley, chopped

½ teaspoon fine sea salt

¼ teaspoon ground black pepper

½ tablespoon cumin

½ tablespoon dried coriander

1¼ teaspoons chili powder

¼ teaspoon turmeric

⅛ teaspoon cayenne pepper

1 egg yolk

¼ cup olive oil, divided

2 whole wheat pitas, cut in half

INSTRUCTIONS:

Falafel Patties

1. Bring the water to a boil. Add the quinoa, reduce the heat to low, cover, and simmer for 15 to 20 minutes until all the liquid is absorbed. Set aside.

2. Preheat the oven to 375°F.

3. Pulse together the chickpeas, onion, garlic, parsley, salt, pepper, and other spices in a food processor. Process until everything is finely chopped (it won't become completely smooth, and that's okay). Transfer to a bowl, and mix in the quinoa. Add the egg yolk and stir until fully incorporated.

4. Shape the dough into eight balls, and then flatten with your palm into about ½-inch-thick patties. Transfer to a parchment-lined cookie sheet.

5. Bake for 10 minutes. Remove from the oven, flip each patty, and bake for another 10 minutes.

6. Heat half of the oil in a large nonstick fry pan. Place four of the patties in the heated oil and fry for 2 to 3 minutes on each side, until golden brown. Repeat with the remaining oil and remaining patties.

Easy Tzatziki

½ cucumber, peeled and grated

2 cloves garlic, minced

Juice of ¼ small lemon

2 tablespoons olive oil

1 cup 2% plain Greek yogurt

1 teaspoon dried dill

¼ teaspoon kosher salt

¼ teaspoon ground black pepper

Tzatziki

7. Place the grated cucumber in a fine-mesh strainer set over the sink or a bowl, and let drain for 10 to 15 minutes.

8. Combine all the ingredients in a large bowl, and mix well. Taste and adjust the seasoning to your liking.

Assembly

9. Fill each pita half with two falafel patties, tzatziki, and any other toppings you like (I recommend crunchy romaine leaves, tomato slices, and red onion).

NUTRITION INFORMATION PER SERVING (2 FALAFELS)
Calories 359, Calories from Fat 161, Fat (g) 17.9, Saturated Fat (g) 2.7, Protein (g) 10.8, Carbohydrate (g) 41.9, Dietary Fiber (g) 8.1, Cholesterol (mg) 45, Sodium (mg) 563

NUTRITION INFORMATION PER SERVING (¼ OF TZATZIKI):
Calories 111, Calories from Fat 72, Fat (g) 8, Saturated Fat (g) 1.6, Protein (g) 6, Carbohydrate (g) 4, Dietary Fiber (g) 0.3, Cholesterol (mg) 3, Sodium (mg) 145

BUFFALO CHICKPEA SALAD SANDWICH

SERVES 4

Buffalo wraps and sandwiches are one of Ryan's go-to restaurant choices. When we're at home, I like making a vegetarian version so that we both can enjoy the buffalo goodness. These sandwiches are spicy, tangy, quick to put together, and versatile—if you don't like tomatoes or basil, add other veggies. I like to eat these grilled, but they're also tasty when eaten cold and filled with crisp romaine.

INGREDIENTS:

1   (15-ounce) can garbanzo beans, rinsed and drained

¼   cup 2% plain Greek yogurt

1   tablespoon buffalo sauce

2   ounces crumbled goat cheese

1   teaspoon dried dill

2   cloves garlic

½   teaspoon Dijon mustard

⅛   teaspoon fine sea salt (or to taste)

¼   teaspoon chili powder

½   teaspoon paprika

⅛–¼ teaspoon cayenne

1   tablespoon olive oil

¼   red onion, diced

8   slices whole wheat bread

2   medium tomatoes, sliced

Basil leaves (optional)

INSTRUCTIONS:

1. In a large bowl, use a fork to smash the garbanzo beans.

2. In a food processor, combine the yogurt, buffalo sauce, goat cheese, dill, garlic, Dijon, and all of the spices. Process until smooth. Add the oil while the processor is running.

3. Pour the yogurt sauce into the bowl with the beans, and mix in the onion. Stir until combined.

4. Divide the Buffalo Chickpea Salad among four slices of bread. Top with tomatoes, basil, and the remaining bread.

5. Eat cold or grill in a panini press.

NUTRITION INFORMATION PER SERVING:

Calories 324, Calories from Fat 65, Fat (g) 7.2, Saturated Fat (g) 2.9, Protein (g) 18.4, Carbohydrate (g) 47.6, Dietary Fiber (g) 10.3, Cholesterol (mg) 7, Sodium (mg) 480

BLACK BEAN AND GOAT CHEESE QUESADILLAS

SERVES 2

When I was a kid, my picky palate usually resulted in me ordering plain cheese quesadillas at restaurants. I still like my quesadillas to be creamy, but now I also want some texture, spice, and variation in flavor. With two types of cheese, spiced black beans, and a tangy sour cream and Greek yogurt sauce, these quesadillas are hearty, cheesy, and totally comforting.

INGREDIENTS:

1 cup no-salt-added black beans, drained and rinsed

¼–½ teaspoon fine sea salt (or to taste), divided

⅛–¼ teaspoon crushed red pepper, divided

½ cup fresh cilantro, chopped, divided

½ cup 2% plain Greek yogurt

2 tablespoons sour cream

¼ teaspoon onion powder

¼ teaspoon garlic powder

2 whole wheat tortillas

2 ounces goat cheese

1 ounce Fontina cheese, shredded (¼ cup)

2 teaspoons olive oil, divided

INSTRUCTIONS:

1. In a large bowl, lightly mash the black beans with a fork and then stir in half the salt, crushed red pepper, and cilantro. Set aside.

2. In another bowl, combine the Greek yogurt, sour cream, onion powder, garlic powder, and remaining salt.

3. Spoon half of the Greek yogurt mixture on one tortilla. Spoon half the black bean mixture on half of the tortilla, and sprinkle with half of the goat cheese and Fontina cheese. Fold the tortilla over and press down. Repeat with the other tortilla and remaining ingredients.

4. Heat ½ teaspoon of the olive oil in a nonstick skillet. Place a tortilla in the skillet. After 2 to 3 minutes, lift the quesadilla, add another ½ teaspoon of olive oil, and cook the other side of the quesadilla until golden brown. Repeat with the remaining tortilla and oil.

5. Top with cilantro, salsa, or sour cream.

NUTRITION INFORMATION PER SERVING:
Calories 515, Calories from Fat 210, Fat (g) 23.3, Saturated Fat (g) 12.5, Protein (g) 29.4, Carbohydrate (g) 47.4, Dietary Fiber (g) 7.6, Cholesterol (mg) 57, Sodium (mg) 676

FRESH VEGGIE AND QUINOA WRAP WITH SUN-DRIED TOMATO AIOLI

SERVES 5

This healthy wrap is based on one of my favorite restaurant meals. It's full of texture from quinoa, carrots, and cashews, and a smooth (vegan!) sun-dried tomato aioli adds creaminess and tons of flavor. The combination of fiber-filled veggies and protein-packed quinoa and tofu makes this a tasty lunch option that will keep you full throughout the afternoon.

INGREDIENTS:

Veggie Quinoa Wrap

½   tablespoon olive oil

1   clove garlic, minced

1   cup tricolor quinoa

2   cups reduced-sodium vegetable broth

1   cup packed spinach, chopped

1   cup packed romaine leaves, chopped

1   cup grated carrot

½   cup alfalfa sprouts

2   tablespoons chopped fresh basil

3   tablespoons unsalted roasted cashews, chopped

1   tablespoon Dijon mustard

5   whole-grain tortillas

INSTRUCTIONS:

Filling

1. Pour the olive oil and garlic in a saucepan over medium heat. When you start to smell the garlic cooking, add the quinoa and toast for a few minutes. Pour in the broth, bring to a boil, and then reduce to a simmer and cover for 15 to 20 minutes. Allow to cool.

2. Stir the spinach, romaine, carrot, sprouts, basil, cashews, and mustard into the cooled quinoa. Taste it to assess the salt and spice level. If you want to add more, go for it.

Aioli

3. Soak the sun-dried tomatoes in water for 5 minutes. After they're loosened up, drain, place in a food processor, and pulse until finely chopped. Add the tofu, basil, lemon, and spices, and process until smooth. Slowly add the oil with the processor running.

NUTRITION INFORMATION PER SERVING:
Calories 431, Calories from Fat 177, Fat (g) 19.6, Saturated Fat (g) 2.8, Protein (g) 14.8, Carbohydrate (g) 52.3, Dietary Fiber (g) 7.7, Cholesterol (mg) 0, Sodium (mg) 659

Vegan Sun-Dried Tomato Aioli

½ cup sun-dried tomatoes (not in oil)

1 (16-ounce) container silken tofu

3–4 fresh basil leaves

2 tablespoons fresh lemon juice

⅛–¼ teaspoon salt (or to taste)

¼ teaspoon ground pepper

⅛ teaspoon ground cayenne (optional)

¼ cup extra-virgin olive oil

Assembly

4. Spread a couple of heaping spoonfuls of aioli onto a tortilla, then top with a couple scoops of the quinoa/veggie filling.

5. Fold two sides into the middle, then wrap, keeping it as tight as possible. Cut in half.

CHAPTER FIVE

SKILLETS, BAKES, AND CASSEROLES

20-MINUTE ENCHILADA SKILLET

SERVES 6

I've made this dish several times, but its flavor and simplicity continue to blow my mind. I prepare a variation of it almost every week, because it makes the perfect heat-and-eat lunch. This recipe is packed with zucchini, bell peppers, and corn, but you can easily swap those with your favorite veggies. I've even made this vegan with nondairy cheese and cashew sour cream and it's been a big hit!

INGREDIENTS:

3   tablespoons olive oil

3   cloves garlic, minced

½   red onion, chopped

⅛   teaspoon fine sea salt (or to taste)

2   small zucchini, sliced

½   red bell pepper, chopped

½   green bell pepper, chopped

¼   teaspoon ground black pepper (or to taste)

1   teaspoon ground cumin

1   teaspoon dried oregano

1   (15-ounce) can organic corn or hominy

1   (15-ounce) can no-salt-added black beans

6   small corn tortillas, cut in half, and then cut into ½-inch strips

2½ cups enchilada sauce, canned or homemade

6   ounces (about 1½ cups) shredded sharp cheddar, divided

INSTRUCTIONS:

1. Set the oven to broil.

2. Heat the olive oil in a large oven-safe skillet.

3. Add the garlic and cook for about 30 seconds over medium heat, then toss in the onion and salt. Cook the onion until translucent and soft, about 3 minutes.

4. Add the zucchini, red bell pepper, green bell pepper, pepper, cumin, and oregano. Cook for about 5 minutes, until all of the veggies are slightly soft but still have a little bite. Toss in the corn, black beans, tortilla strips, enchilada sauce, and half of the cheese. Stir until fully combined, then top with the remaining cheese.

5. Place the skillet in the oven and broil for 3 to 5 minutes, until the skillet is bubbly and the cheese is melted.

6. Serve with fresh cilantro and a dollop of sour cream.

NUTRITION INFORMATION PER SERVING:
Calories 401, Calories from Fat 177, Fat (g) 19.7, Saturated Fat (g) 7.2, Protein (g) 15, Carbohydrate (g) 41.7, Dietary Fiber (g) 7.9, Cholesterol (mg) 30, Sodium (mg) 688

SWEET-AND-SOUR STIR-FRY WITH BROILED TOFU

SERVES 4

I strongly believe that sweet-and-sour sauce makes everything better. The magical sauce is actually really easy to throw together, and works both as a marinade and a stir-fry sauce in this dish. Broiling the sweet-and-sour tofu results in a gloss on the outside, char on the edges, and a hearty, chewy texture inside.

INGREDIENTS:

Sweet-and-Sour Sauce

1   tablespoon cornstarch

1   tablespoon water

¾   cup pineapple juice

⅓   cup brown rice vinegar

¼   cup packed dark brown sugar

3   tablespoons ketchup

1   tablespoon low-sodium soy sauce

Stir-Fry

1   (14-ounce) block extra-firm tofu, cut into eight 3½ x ½-inch strips

1   tablespoon vegetable oil

2   cloves garlic, minced

1   yellow onion, chopped

½   green onion, chopped

½   red onion, chopped

1   green bell pepper, chopped

1   red bell pepper, chopped

1   cup brown rice, for serving

NUTRITION INFORMATION PER SERVING:
Calories 461, Calories from Fat 105, Fat (g) 11.7, Saturated Fat (g) 1.2, Protein (g) 17.2, Carbohydrate (g) 75.5, Dietary Fiber (g) 5.5, Cholesterol (mg) 0, Sodium (mg) 287

INSTRUCTIONS:

1. Whisk together the cornstarch and water. Set aside.

2. Bring the pineapple juice, vinegar, sugar, ketchup, and soy sauce to a boil in a medium saucepan.

3. Pour in the cornstarch mixture and cook for another 1 to 2 minutes, until thickened. Set aside. Set the oven to broil.

4. Dip the tofu slices in the sweet-and-sour mixture. Place on a greased baking sheet, and set the sheet on an oven rack in the upper third of your oven. Broil for 5 minutes, flip, brush with more sweet-and-sour sauce, and broil for another 5 minutes. Flip one more time, brush on more sauce, and broil for 3 more minutes, until the edges have a slight char and the tofu is glossy. Watch carefully as you broil the tofu, since all ovens are different, and there's a fine line between broiled and burned.

5. While the tofu broils, heat the vegetable oil in a large skillet. Add the garlic and cook until fragrant. Pour in the onions and stir for 3 to 5 minutes, until softened. Add the peppers and cook for another 5 to 7 minutes, until softened.

6. Cook the brown rice according to the package directions.

7. Serve a quarter of the vegetables and rice with two slices of broiled tofu.

BRUSSELS SPROUT QUINOA GRATIN

SERVES 6

I love brussels sprouts in all shapes and forms, but this might just be the best way to eat my favorite mini cabbages. This recipe mixes lightly roasted brussels sprouts with a super-creamy and cheesy sauce, quinoa, and crispy bread crumbs. I like to make a big batch of this gratin on Sundays so I can eat it all week, but I've also brought it to holiday dinners with rave reviews from each member of my very picky and particular family.

INGREDIENTS:

2   cups water

1   cup quinoa, uncooked

1   pound brussels sprouts, quartered

1   tablespoon olive oil, divided

1   tablespoon fresh thyme leaves

2   teaspoons dried parsley

2   tablespoons butter

2   tablespoons all-purpose flour

2   cups low-fat milk

4   ounces (about 1 cup) Gruyère, shredded

2   ounces (about ½ cup) Fontina, shredded

¾   teaspoon kosher salt, or to taste

½   teaspoon ground pepper

⅛   teaspoon ground nutmeg

1   teaspoon garlic, minced

1   slice whole wheat bread, processed into crumbs

2   tablespoons grated Parmesan cheese

INSTRUCTIONS:

1. Preheat the oven to 375°F.

2. Bring the water to a boil. Add the quinoa, reduce the heat to low, cover, and simmer for 15 to 20 minutes, until all the liquid is absorbed.

3. Toss the brussels sprouts with ½ tablespoon of the olive oil and roast in the oven for 10 to 15 minutes, until just starting to brown. They will continue to cook in the gratin, so you don't want to overcook them at this stage.

4. Reduce the oven heat to 350°F.

5. Toss the roasted sprouts with the quinoa, thyme, and parsley.

6. For the sauce, melt the butter over medium heat, then whisk in the flour. Pour the milk into the saucepan, bring to a light boil, and whisk constantly for 5 minutes until thickened.

7. Remove the sauce from the heat and stir in the Gruyère, Fontina, salt, pepper, and nutmeg. Stir into the quinoa-sprout mixture.

8. Heat the remaining ½ tablespoon of olive oil over medium heat, then add the garlic and cook until fragrant. Stir in the bread crumbs and cook for 2 to 3 minutes, until slightly browned and crisp.

9. Pour the quinoa-sprout mixture into an 8 x 8-inch dish, then sprinkle with the Parmesan and bread crumbs.

10. Bake uncovered for 25 to 30 minutes, until the top is golden. Allow to cool for 10 minutes before cutting in.

NUTRITION INFORMATION PER SERVING:
Calories 353, Calories from Fat 155, Fat (g) 17.2, Saturated Fat (g) 8.3, Protein (g) 17.5, Carbohydrate (g) 34.1, Dietary Fiber (g) 4.8, Cholesterol (mg) 42, Sodium (mg) 442

BUTTERNUT SQUASH, BARLEY, AND CHEDDAR BAKE

SERVES 6

There are few things I find more comforting than main dishes that include warm, golden, and melty cheese. In this casserole, you get the mixture of plump pearl barley, lightly sweet butternut squash, and a rich and flavorful sharp cheddar and rosemary sauce. This dish is so decadent tasting *and* it's filled with whole grains (pearl barley), vitamin A (butternut squash), and protein.

INGREDIENTS:

1   cup uncooked pearl barley

3   cups water

2   tablespoons olive oil

2   cloves garlic, minced

½   red onion, diced

3½ cups cubed butternut squash

2   tablespoons butter

2   tablespoons unbleached all-purpose flour

2   cups 1% milk, room temperature

½   teaspoon fine sea salt

¼   teaspoon black pepper

2   teaspoons dried rosemary

⅛   teaspoon freshly grated nutmeg

4   ounces extra-sharp cheddar cheese, shredded (about 1 cup)

3   ounces Parmesan cheese, shredded (about ¾ cup)

INSTRUCTIONS:

1. Preheat the oven to 350°F.

2. Combine the barley and water. Bring to a boil, reduce to a simmer, and cover for 35 to 40 minutes, until most of the water is absorbed. Drain any remaining water.

3. While the barley is cooking, heat the olive oil in a large fry pan. Add the garlic and cook for 30 seconds over medium heat, until fragrant. Add the onion and cook for another 3 minutes, until translucent. Pour in the squash and cook for 10 minutes, stirring occasionally, until the squash is just fork-tender.

4. While the squash cooks, melt the butter in a separate saucepan. Whisk in the flour and cook for 30 to 45 seconds, until it forms a paste. Pour in the milk, salt, pepper, rosemary, and nutmeg, and bring to a boil. Whisk constantly for 5 minutes until the sauce thickens. Remove from the heat and stir in the cheddar until smooth.

5. In a large bowl, combine the barley, squash, and cheese sauce. Stir until the sauce is well distributed. Pour into an 8 x 8-inch baking dish, then top with the Parmesan. Cover with aluminum foil and bake for 25 minutes. Uncover, put the oven on broil, and broil for 5 minutes, until the top is golden.

6. Allow to sit for 10 minutes before serving.

NUTRITION INFORMATION PER SERVING:
Calories 414, Calories from Fat 177, Fat (g) 19.7, Saturated Fat (g) 10, Protein (g) 17.2, Carbohydrate (g) 44.5, Dietary Fiber (g) 7.5, Cholesterol (mg) 44, Sodium (mg) 585

The High-Protein Vegetarian Cookbook

MEXICAN FAJITA PIE

SERVES 6

It's easy to run to a local restaurant when the Mexican craving hits, but if you get that craving as often as I do, you need a solid homemade recipe go to. This Mexican Fajita Pie is loaded with protein from two types of beans (black and refried), whole wheat tortillas, and sharp cheddar. Bell peppers spiced with oregano, cumin, and chili powder add a boost in flavor and texture. The result? One serious fix for your Mexican craving.

INGREDIENTS:

- 1 (15-ounce) can vegetarian refried beans
- ½ cup salsa
- 2 tablespoons sour cream
- 2 tablespoons olive oil
- 1 clove garlic, minced
- ½ red onion, thinly sliced
- 1 red pepper, thinly sliced
- 1 green pepper, thinly sliced
- ¼ teaspoon fine sea salt
- 1 teaspoon dried oregano
- 1 teaspoon cumin
- 1 teaspoon chili powder
- 1 cup black beans, drained and rinsed
- 4 whole wheat tortillas
- 6 ounces sharp cheddar cheese, shredded (about 1½ cups)

INSTRUCTIONS:

1. Preheat the oven to 400°F.

2. Combine the refried beans with the salsa and sour cream in a large bowl. Set aside.

3. Heat the olive oil in a large skillet over medium heat. Add the garlic and cook until fragrant. Add the onion, red pepper, green pepper, salt, and spices. Cook until all are softened, about 10 minutes.

4. Remove the pan from the heat and stir in the black beans.

5. Place a tortilla on the bottom of a 9-inch round cake pan. Top with a quarter of the refried bean mixture, a third of the stir-fried vegetables, and ¼ cup of the cheese. Repeat two more times, then top with the last flour tortilla, remaining refried beans, and remaining ½ cup cheese.

6. Cover with foil and bake for 30 minutes. Remove the foil and broil for 2 to 3 minutes, until the cheese on top is golden.

7. Let sit for 10 minutes before cutting.

NUTRITION INFORMATION PER SERVING:
Calories 395, Calories from Fat 157, Fat (g) 17.5, Saturated Fat (g) 7.3, Protein (g) 17.8, Carbohydrate (g) 43.5, Dietary Fiber (g) 9.3, Cholesterol (mg) 33, Sodium (mg) 630

BROCCOLI-AND-BARLEY-STUFFED BELL PEPPERS

SERVES 8

Although most stuffed pepper recipes are full of protein from ground beef, this vegetarian version packs loads of protein, nutrients, and texture with barley, broccoli, and mozzarella. Fresh basil and juicy grape tomatoes give each bite a caprese Italian flavor. To save on time, you can make the barley the night before, and then throw these peppers together for a quick weeknight dinner.

INGREDIENTS:

Stuffed Peppers

1 cup pearl barley, uncooked

3 cups low-sodium vegetable broth

4 large bell peppers (I used a variety of colors)

1 tablespoon olive oil

2 cloves garlic, minced

2 shallots, diced

½ teaspoon kosher salt

1½ cups broccoli florets, stems removed and roughly chopped

1 cup grape tomatoes, quartered

½ cup fresh basil leaves, chopped

2 ounces mozzarella, shredded (about ½ cup)

4 ounces fresh mozzarella, sliced

Easy Marinara

2 tablespoons olive oil

1 clove garlic, minced

1 (28.2-ounce) can no-salt-added crushed tomatoes

½ teaspoon kosher salt

¼ teaspoon crushed red pepper

2 tablespoons chopped fresh basil

½ tablespoon brown sugar

INSTRUCTIONS:

1. Combine the barley and broth in a saucepan. Bring to a boil. Reduce the heat to low and simmer, covered, for 40 to 45 minutes.

2. Preheat the oven to 350°F.

3. Cut the peppers in half and scoop out the seeds and ribs. I like to keep the top of the stem on, because it helps keep the filling from spilling out.

4. Bring a large pot of water to a boil. Add the peppers, bring the water back up to a boil, and boil for 3 minutes. Remove from the pot and set aside.

5. Heat 1 tablespoon of olive oil in a large pan over medium heat. Add the garlic and cook until fragrant (about 30 seconds). Add the shallots and salt, then cook for 2 to 3 minutes. Add the broccoli and grape tomatoes, and cook until the broccoli is bright green and the tomatoes are starting to get soft (about 5 minutes). Transfer to a large bowl, then pour in the cooked barley, and add the basil and shredded mozzarella.

6. Place the boiled peppers in a 9 x 13-inch baking dish filled with ½ cup of water. Stuff each pepper with filling. To make the most of the filling, push the filling down into the pepper and allow it to heap over the top of the pepper. Top each pepper with a slice of fresh mozzarella. Bake for 35 minutes.

7. While they are baking, make the marinara. Heat the olive oil over medium heat, add the garlic, and cook until fragrant. Pour in the tomatoes, salt, red pepper flakes, fresh basil, and brown sugar. Bring to a boil, then reduce to a simmer and let the mixture cook for 15 minutes.

8. When the peppers are done baking, pour the sauce over them and top with more fresh basil (if desired).

NUTRITION INFORMATION PER SERVING (½ OF 1 PEPPER AND ⅛ OF MARINARA):

Calories 273, Calories from Fat 90, Fat (g) 10, Saturated Fat (g) 2.5, Protein (g) 10.2, Carbohydrate (g) 35.7, Dietary Fiber (g) 8.6, Cholesterol (mg) 9, Sodium (mg) 397

SPINACH ARTICHOKE LASAGNA ROLL-UPS

SERVES 9

These rich and creamy lasagna rolls are reminiscent of my favorite restaurant dip! Each roll is filled with chopped spinach and artichokes, and cloaked in a thick and cheesy sauce. Protein-filled low-fat dairy, including cottage cheese and Greek yogurt, packs each roll with protein, while four varieties of cheese make for a comforting, crowd-pleasing meal.

INGREDIENTS:

9   lasagna noodles, dry

1   tablespoon olive oil

2   cloves garlic, minced

¼   cup finely chopped red onion

¼   teaspoon kosher salt

1   (14-ounce) can artichoke hearts, rinsed and roughly chopped

5   ounces baby spinach, chopped

Juice of ½ lemon

1   cup 1% cottage cheese

½   cup 2% plain Greek yogurt

3   ounces extra-sharp cheddar cheese, shredded (about ¾ cup)

1   ounce Parmesan cheese, shredded (about ¼ cup)

INSTRUCTIONS:

1. Cook the lasagna noodles according to the package directions. Place on a sheet of parchment paper.

2. Preheat the oven to 300°F.

3. Heat the olive oil in a large skillet over medium heat. Add the garlic and cook for 30 seconds. Add the onion, sprinkle with salt, and cook for 2 to 3 minutes, until translucent. Pour in the artichokes, cook for a minute, then add the spinach and lemon juice and cook until the spinach is wilted. Transfer to a mixing bowl and drain the excess liquid.

4. Puree the cottage cheese in a blender or food processor until smooth and creamy.

5. Add the cottage cheese, Greek yogurt, cheddar, and Parmesan to the spinach and artichokes. Mix well.

6. For the Cream Sauce, heat the butter in a medium-sized saucepan over medium heat. Whisk in the flour, and keep whisking until it forms a paste. Pour in the milk, nutmeg, salt, and pepper. Whisk continuously for 5 to 7 minutes, until the sauce has thickened. Remove from the heat and stir in the cheeses until smooth.

7. Spread some of the spinach-artichoke mixture on each noodle. Roll up carefully.

Cream Sauce

2 tablespoons unsalted butter

2 tablespoons unbleached all-purpose flour

3 cups 1% milk

¼ teaspoon freshly grated nutmeg

¼ teaspoon kosher salt

¼ teaspoon black pepper

3 ounces cream cheese

2 ounces Parmesan cheese, shredded (about ½ cup)

2 ounces mozzarella, shredded (about ½ cup)

8. Ladle ¾ cup of sauce on the bottom of a 9 x 13-inch cake pan. Place the rolls seam-side down in the pan, then top with the remaining sauce. Cover with aluminum foil and cook for 40 minutes.

9. To serve, place each roll on a plate and then spoon on additional sauce from the pan, as desired.

NUTRITION INFORMATION PER SERVING:

Calories 323, Calories from Fat 134, Fat (g) 14.9, Saturated Fat (g) 8.2, Protein (g) 18.3, Carbohydrate (g) 29, Dietary Fiber (g) 2.6, Cholesterol (mg) 41, Sodium (mg) 564

VEGAN ROASTED VEGETABLE LASAGNA

SERVES 6

Vegan lasagna might sound crazy to cheese-lovers around the world (there was definitely a time when it seemed crazy to me), but it really can be just as satisfying as the full-dairy version. This recipe roasts vegetables to make them extra flavorful and sweet, then layers them with whole wheat lasagna noodles and a filling made of cashews, crumbled tofu, and spices. The resulting lasagna is flavorful, packed with texture, and full of protein and fiber.

INGREDIENTS:

Filling

½   cup unsalted roasted cashews

¼   cup nutritional yeast

2   cloves garlic, chopped

1   teaspoon dried oregano

1   teaspoon dried basil

¼   teaspoon fine sea salt

1   (14-ounce) container extra-firm tofu

Roasted Vegetables

1   zucchini, cut into ½-inch pieces

1   red bell pepper, cut into ½-inch pieces

8   ounces sliced white mushrooms

½   yellow onion, cut into ½-inch pieces

1   tablespoon olive oil

¼   teaspoon fine sea salt

¼   teaspoon ground black pepper

NUTRITION INFORMATION PER SERVING:
Calories 387, Calories from Fat 140, Fat (g) 15.6, Saturated Fat (g) 2.3, Protein (g) 20.8, Carbohydrate (g) 43.8, Dietary Fiber (g) 8.4, Cholesterol (mg) 0, Sodium (mg) 468

INSTRUCTIONS:

Filling

1. Pour boiling-hot water over the cashews, and let them sit for 45 minutes.

2. Once they're done softening in the water, place them in a food processor with the nutritional yeast, garlic, oregano, basil, and sea salt. Process until all the ingredients are very finely chopped. Transfer the ingredients to a bowl.

3. Use your fingers to crumble in the tofu. Stir to combine.

Veggies

4. Preheat the oven to 400°F.

5. Combine all the vegetables in a bowl. Pour in the olive oil, salt, and pepper, and toss to combine. Spread in one layer on a baking sheet, and roast for 20 to 25 minutes.

Sauce

6. Heat the olive oil in a medium pot over medium heat.

7. Add the garlic and cook for 30 seconds, then add the tomatoes, tomato paste, salt, oregano, basil, and red pepper.

8. Bring to a boil, then reduce the heat to low, cover, and simmer for 15 minutes.

Sauce

1 tablespoon olive oil

2 cloves garlic, minced

1 (28-ounce) can crushed tomatoes with basil

2 tablespoons tomato paste

½ teaspoon fine sea salt

1 teaspoon dried oregano

1 teaspoon dried basil

¼ teaspoon crushed red pepper

Assembly

8 whole wheat lasagna noodles

Fresh basil, for garnish

Assembly

9. Preheat the oven to 350°F.

10. Cook the lasagna noodles according to the package directions.

11. Spread ¼ cup of sauce in an 8 x 8-inch square baking dish. Top with two lasagna noodles. Spread a quarter of the tofu-cashew filling on top of the noodles, then a third of the veggies, followed by ½ cup of the sauce. Repeat this layering twice, then top with two more noodles and the last of the tofu-cashew filling and sauce.

12. Cover with foil and bake for 40 minutes. Remove the foil and bake for another 10 minutes.

13. Let sit for 10 minutes before cutting. Slice into six pieces, and serve with sliced fresh basil on top.

SAVORY SIDES AND APPETIZERS

WHITE CHEDDAR CORN BREAD MUFFINS

SERVES 12

It took a long time for me to love corn bread, but the sweet-and-salty combo has finally found its place in my heart. These muffins are made with whole wheat flour, less butter than typical corn bread recipes, and protein-packed Greek yogurt. They're soft, flavorful, and perfect when slightly warmed and drizzled with honey.

INGREDIENTS:

¼ cup unsalted butter, softened

½ cup 0% plain Greek yogurt

2 tablespoons granulated sugar

2 large eggs

¾ cup low-fat buttermilk

1½ cups white whole wheat flour

¾ cup yellow cornmeal

1 teaspoon baking soda

1¼ teaspoons fine sea salt

½ cup corn kernels (from a can or frozen and thawed)

4 ounces sharp white cheddar, shredded (about 1 cup)

INSTRUCTIONS:

1. Preheat the oven to 400°F.

2. Beat together the butter, Greek yogurt, and sugar in a large bowl until creamy (3 to 5 minutes). Mix in the eggs and buttermilk.

3. In another bowl, whisk together the flour, cornmeal, baking soda, and salt.

4. Gradually stir the dry ingredients into the wet ingredients.

5. Fold in the corn and cheese.

6. Divide the batter among 12 lined and greased muffin tins. Bake for 20 to 25 minutes, until the tops are golden and a toothpick inserted in the center comes out clean.

NUTRITION INFORMATION PER SERVING:
Calories 195, Calories from Fat 75, Fat (g) 8.4, Saturated Fat (g) 4.9, Protein (g) 7.7, Carbohydrate (g) 23.9, Dietary Fiber (g) 1.8, Cholesterol (mg) 52, Sodium (mg) 442

ROSEMARY PARMESAN DROP BISCUITS

SERVES 12

I'm a big fan of drop biscuits because they're quick and easy, while still appearing (and tasting) impressive. I brought this rosemary and Parmesan version to my family's Thanksgiving last year and they were a huge hit. They're a good source of protein thanks to the Greek yogurt, Parmesan, and whole wheat, but all your dinner guests will care about is their fluffy texture and buttery taste.

INGREDIENTS:

1½ cups unbleached all-purpose flour

¾ cup whole wheat flour

1 teaspoon baking powder

1 teaspoon baking soda

1 teaspoon kosher salt

¼ teaspoon black pepper

½ teaspoon sugar

5 tablespoons fresh rosemary, chopped, divided

6 tablespoons very cold unsalted butter, cut into small cubes

⅔ cup plus 2 tablespoons grated Parmesan cheese, divided

1 cup low-fat buttermilk

½ cup 2% plain Greek yogurt

1 tablespoon olive oil

INSTRUCTIONS:

1. Preheat the oven to 375°F.

2. Whisk together the flours, baking powder, baking soda, salt, pepper, sugar, and 3 tablespoons of the rosemary.

3. Cut in the butter pieces, using a pastry blender or your hands to incorporate it until you only have pea-sized pieces of butter left.

4. Stir in ⅔ cup of the Parmesan. In a separate bowl, combine the buttermilk and yogurt. Pour it into the dry ingredients and stir just until combined.

5. Drop ¼ cupfuls of dough onto parchment-lined baking sheets. These biscuits get much larger as they bake, so I recommend dividing the dough across two baking sheets so they have room to expand.

6. Sprinkle each biscuit with remaining Parmesan, rosemary, and a drizzle of olive oil. Bake for 15 to 20 minutes, until golden on top.

NUTRITION INFORMATION PER SERVING:
Calories 179, Calories from Fat 80, Fat (g) 8.9, Saturated Fat (g) 4.9, Protein (g) 6, Carbohydrate (g) 19.3, Dietary Fiber (g) 1.3, Cholesterol (mg) 20, Sodium (mg) 398

SPANISH QUINOA

SERVES 4

Ryan and I make Mexican food frequently, and no matter what we eat we always serve it with our favorite side: Spanish quinoa. This recipe is every bit as flavorful as Spanish rice, but it's full of fiber, protein, and whole-grain goodness.

INGREDIENTS:

1   tablespoon olive oil

½   red onion, diced

1   cup quinoa

1¾ cups vegetable broth

1   (14.5-ounce) can no-salt-added diced tomatoes

¼   cup fresh cilantro, chopped

¼–½ teaspoon crushed red pepper

INSTRUCTIONS:

1. Heat the olive oil in a medium-sized saucepan over medium heat. Add the red onion and cook until softened and translucent (2 to 3 minutes).

2. Add the quinoa and stir for 2 to 3 minutes until the quinoa is toasted.

3. Pour in the vegetable broth, tomatoes, cilantro, and red pepper flakes. Bring to a boil, then reduce to a simmer for 20 to 25 minutes, until the liquid is absorbed.

NUTRITION INFORMATION PER SERVING:
Calories 229, Calories from Fat 56, Fat (g) 6.3, Saturated Fat (g) 0.8, Protein (g) 7.6, Carbohydrate (g) 37.6, Dietary Fiber (g) 5.1, Cholesterol (mg) 0, Sodium (mg) 468

LEMON MILLET WITH ASPARAGUS AND GREEN PEAS

SERVES 6

When springtime rolls around, all I want to eat is asparagus with lemon. Since spring in Minnesota tends to come late, I turn to this bright and fresh combination so I can at least get a taste of the season. This dish combines my favorite flavors with chewy millet and green peas. Adding a touch of goat cheese to the warm grains results in a creamy, tangy side dish.

INGREDIENTS:

1   cup hulled millet

2   cups vegetable broth

¼   cup fresh lemon juice

1½   teaspoons dried thyme, divided

20   asparagus spears, tough ends removed, then chopped into 1-inch pieces

1⅓   cups frozen green peas

1½   tablespoons olive oil

¼   teaspoon fine sea salt

1   ounce (¼ cup) crumbled goat cheese

INSTRUCTIONS:

1. Place the millet in a saucepan and toast for 3 to 5 minutes. Pour in the broth, lemon juice, and thyme, and bring to a boil. Reduce the heat to low and simmer for 20 to 25 minutes, until most of the liquid is absorbed. Keep covered and set aside for 10 minutes so the millet can absorb the remainder of the broth.

2. While the millet cooks, prepare the vegetables. Preheat the oven to 400°F. Toss the asparagus and green peas with the olive oil and salt. Spread on a baking sheet and bake for 8 minutes, then turn the oven to broil and broil for 2 minutes, until the peas and asparagus are lightly golden.

3. Combine the cooked millet, asparagus, and peas. Stir in the goat cheese while all the ingredients are still warm.

NUTRITION INFORMATION PER SERVING:
Calories 217, Calories from Fat 54, Fat (g) 6, Saturated Fat (g) 1.4, Protein (g) 7.7, Carbohydrate (g) 33.8, Dietary Fiber (g) 6.4, Cholesterol (mg) 2, Sodium (mg) 169

ROASTED GARLIC BUTTERNUT SQUASH HUMMUS

SERVES 8

If you're a fan of sweet-and-savory snacking, this is the hummus for you. Rosemary-roasted butternut squash and garlic bring depth of flavor to this chickpea dip, while protein-rich ricotta makes the texture light and fluffy. Serve this hummus with pita or crackers, or as a spread on sandwiches or homemade veggie burgers.

INGREDIENTS:

- 2 tablespoons olive oil, divided
- 1 medium-sized butternut squash (2 pounds), peeled, seeded, and cut into 1-inch cubes
- 4 cloves garlic
- 1 tablespoon dried rosemary
- 1 (15-ounce) can chickpeas, drained and rinsed
- 1 teaspoon paprika
- 1 teaspoon chili powder
- ¼ teaspoon ground cayenne pepper
- ¾ teaspoon fine sea salt
- ¼ teaspoon black pepper
- ¾ cup part-skim ricotta cheese

INSTRUCTIONS:

1. Preheat the oven to 400°F.

2. Drizzle 1 tablespoon of the olive oil over the butternut squash and garlic. Stir until it coats everything evenly. Wrap the cloves in aluminum foil, then stir the dried rosemary into the squash.

3. Bake for 25 to 30 minutes, until the squash is fork-tender. Set aside and allow to cool.

4. In a food processor, combine the squash, garlic, chickpeas, paprika, chili powder, cayenne, salt, and pepper. Process until smooth, then pour in the remaining olive oil while it's running.

5. Add the ricotta and process again until smooth.

NUTRITION INFORMATION PER SERVING:
Calories 156, Calories from Fat 57, Fat (g) 6.3, Saturated Fat (g) 1.8, Protein (g) 6.6, Carbohydrate (g) 20.1, Dietary Fiber (g) 4.5, Cholesterol (mg) 7, Sodium (mg) 259

SPINACH ARTICHOKE DIP

SERVES 9

Indulging in game-day snacks does not mean that you have to fill up on low-protein foods. This recipe is every bit as creamy and addicting as a dip you'd order at a restaurant, but the hidden tofu and Greek yogurt sneakily add protein and replace some of the higher-fat ingredients. The first time I made this, Ryan and I ended up eating the entire pan all by ourselves in just 2 days—scooping it up with chips, smothering it on bread, and even using it as a veggie dip.

INGREDIENTS:

- 2 tablespoons olive oil
- 3 cloves garlic, minced
- ½ yellow onion, chopped
- 1 (12-ounce) bag frozen artichokes, thawed and roughly chopped
- 1 jalapeño, seeded and chopped
- ¾ teaspoon fine sea salt, divided
- 4 cups fresh spinach (5-ounce container)
- 12 ounces silken tofu
- 3 ounces light cream cheese, softened
- ½ cup 2% plain Greek yogurt
- 2 ounces sharp white cheddar cheese, shredded
- 2 ounces feta, crumbled
- 2 ounces Parmesan cheese, shredded (about ½ cup)
- ¼ teaspoon black pepper
- 2 tablespoons chopped fresh basil
- ¼ teaspoon red pepper flakes (or to taste)

INSTRUCTIONS:

1. Preheat the oven to 350°F.

2. Heat the olive oil and garlic in a large saucepan. Once the garlic is fragrant, add the onion and cook until translucent, about 2 to 3 minutes. Add the artichokes, jalapeño, and ½ teaspoon of the salt, then cook until the artichokes are soft, around 4 minutes. Pour in the spinach and cook until it starts to wilt.

3. In a food processor, pulse together the tofu and cream cheese until smooth. Pour into another bowl, then add the Greek yogurt, cheeses, spices, and the remaining salt. Mix the artichoke and spinach into the cheese mixture, then pour into a lightly greased 9-inch pie pan or casserole dish.

4. Cover with aluminum foil and bake for 25 minutes. Uncover and cook for another 5 minutes, then turn the oven to broil and continue to bake for 3 more minutes, until the top becomes golden.

5. Let sit for 10 minutes before digging in, then serve with chips, bread, or veggies.

NUTRITION INFORMATION PER SERVING:

Calories 169, Calories from Fat 102, Fat (g) 11.3, Saturated Fat (g) 5.2, Protein (g) 10.3, Carbohydrate (g) 8.7, Dietary Fiber (g) 3.3, Cholesterol (mg) 22, Sodium (mg) 348

CREAMY ROASTED TOMATO AND BASIL HUMMUS

SERVES 4

I love hummus, but the traditional tahini version can get a bit boring if you eat it day after day. This hummus is easy to whip together and packs tons of flavor with roasted tomatoes, fresh basil, and creamy Greek yogurt. This hummus works great as a dip, but I love layering it on crusty bread with mozzarella and basil, and then grilling it until golden and melty.

INGREDIENTS:

- 2 Roma tomatoes, halved and seeded
- 2 tablespoons plus 1 teaspoon olive oil, divided
- ½ teaspoon kosher salt, divided
- ¼ cup fresh basil leaves
- 2 cloves garlic
- 1 (15-ounce) can chickpeas, drained and rinsed
- ¼ teaspoon ground black pepper
- ¼ cup 2% plain Greek yogurt

INSTRUCTIONS:

1. Preheat the oven to 325°F.

2. Place the tomatoes cut-side down on a baking sheet. Pour 1 teaspoon of the olive oil over the tomatoes and sprinkle with ¼ teaspoon of the salt. Bake for 50 minutes to 1 hour.

3. Place the basil and garlic in a food processor and pulse until finely chopped.

4. Add the roasted tomatoes and process until smooth.

5. Pour in the chickpeas, pepper, and remaining salt. Process again until smooth.

6. Slowly add the remaining olive oil with the processor running.

7. Add the Greek yogurt and pulse until just incorporated.

NUTRITION INFORMATION PER SERVING:
Calories 188, Calories from Fat 88, Fat (g) 9.8, Saturated Fat (g) 1.4, Protein (g) 7.2, Carbohydrate (g) 18.9, Dietary Fiber (g) 5.1, Cholesterol (mg) 1, Sodium (mg) 352

EDAMAME AND AVOCADO DIP

SERVES 5

This dip combines guacamole flavors of avocado, garlic, lime, and cilantro, while the edamame (a.k.a. soybean) base gives it a more robust flavor than your average guacamole. I like to think of it as the love child of hummus and guacamole. It goes great with crackers and tortilla chips, or as a spread for sandwiches.

INGREDIENTS:

2   cloves garlic

¼   cup packed fresh cilantro, plus more for garnish

1½ cups shelled edamame

Juice of ½ lime

¼   teaspoon kosher salt

⅛   teaspoon black pepper

½   large avocado, pitted

½   cup 2% plain Greek yogurt

2   tablespoons extra-virgin olive oil

INSTRUCTIONS:

1. Combine the garlic and cilantro in a food processor, and pulse until very finely chopped. Add all the remaining ingredients, except the olive oil, and process together until smooth. Add the olive oil gradually while the processor is running.

2. Transfer to a bowl and garnish with cilantro.

NUTRITION INFORMATION PER SERVING:
Calories 146, Calories from Fat 93, Fat (g) 10.3, Saturated Fat (g) 1.5, Protein (g) 7, Carbohydrate (g) 7.4, Dietary Fiber (g) 2.9, Cholesterol (mg) 1, Sodium (mg) 113

SPICY ROASTED CHICKPEAS

SERVES 3

I come from a long line of picky eaters, and these chickpeas are one of the only snacks that my whole family can agree on. They're spicy, crunchy, and full of that buffalo flavor that drives people crazy. A touch of buffalo wing sauce serves as the base for the flavor, but additional spices add depth and heat. Roasted chickpeas do not keep their crunch more than a couple of days, but I rarely can keep them around longer than that before I need to make another batch.

INGREDIENTS:

- 1 (15-ounce) can chickpeas, drained and rinsed
- ½ teaspoon buffalo wing sauce
- 1 teaspoon olive oil
- ⅛ teaspoon granulated sugar
- ½ teaspoon garlic powder
- ¼ teaspoon onion powder
- ¼ teaspoon smoked paprika
- ½ teaspoon chili powder
- ¼ teaspoon cumin
- ⅛–¼ teaspoon cayenne
- ¼ teaspoon salt

INSTRUCTIONS:

1. Preheat the oven to 425°F.

2. To ensure that the chickpeas get crispy in the oven, you need to remove as much moisture as possible. Roll them around between paper towels to dry them off. Remove the skins that loosen from the chickpeas—this will help your chickpeas get crunchy.

3. Mix together all of the remaining ingredients in a bowl. Add the chickpeas and stir gently with a spoon until all of them are evenly coated.

4. Spread the chickpeas out onto a parchment-lined cookie sheet.

5. Bake for 25 to 30 minutes, removing from the oven to stir two times.

NUTRITION INFORMATION PER SERVING:
Calories 150, Calories from Fat 33, Fat (g) 3.7, Saturated Fat (g) 0.4, Protein (g) 7.3, Carbohydrate (g) 23.1, Dietary Fiber (g) 6.4, Cholesterol (mg) 0, Sodium (mg) 359

ROASTED CORN AND CANNELLINI BEAN DIP

SERVES 12

Ryan has a reputation among his friends of loving corn more than any other human on the planet. They claim to have seen him devour eight ears in one sitting. I, on the other hand, am a little picky about my corn; I only like it roasted. Roasting corn kernels brings out their sweetness, which in this case goes well with creamy cannellini beans and tangy cream cheese. We devoured this dip when I made it for the Super Bowl, and I ended up making it a week later because we craved more!

INGREDIENTS:

1½ cups frozen corn kernels

2 cloves garlic, minced

1 tablespoon olive oil

1 (15-ounce) can cannellini beans

¾ teaspoon fine sea salt

1 teaspoon dried oregano

4 ounces light cream cheese, softened

4 ounces part-skim mozzarella, shredded (about 1 cup)

¼ cup grated Parmesan cheese, divided

NUTRITION INFORMATION PER SERVING:
Calories 107, Calories from Fat 45, Fat (g) 5, Saturated Fat (g) 2.6, Protein (g) 6.1, Carbohydrate (g) 11.1, Dietary Fiber (g) 3, Cholesterol (mg) 12, Sodium (mg) 257

INSTRUCTIONS:

1. Preheat the oven to 450°F.

2. Toss the corn and garlic cloves with the olive oil, and place on a baking sheet. Roast for 10 to 12 minutes, until just lightly browned. You don't want them to be crispy, so stop baking when they begin to look golden.

3. Lower the oven temperature to 350°F.

4. Set aside ½ cup of corn kernels, then place the remaining corn in a food processor with the beans, salt, and oregano. Process until mostly smooth. Add the cream cheese and pulse a few times, until just incorporated.

5. Transfer the bean and corn mixture to a large bowl, and fold in the remaining kernels, mozzarella, and half the Parmesan.

6. Spoon the dip into an 8- or 9-inch round casserole dish. Top with the remaining Parmesan. Bake for 20 to 25 minutes, and then broil for 2 to 3 minutes until the top becomes golden.

7. Let sit for 5 minutes before serving, and then serve with pita, crusty bread, or crackers.

BUFFALO QUINOA BITES WITH FETA RANCH

SERVES 10

Truth be told, finger foods are one of the only reasons I ever watch football. Although the usual football fare tends to be meat-heavy, I find that incorporating buffalo sauce usually results in a big hit with most sports crowds. These bites combine that magical sauce with quinoa, red lentils, and tons of spices. The buffalo bites aren't overly spicy, but they do taste even better with the tangy, cooling Feta Ranch dipping sauce.

INGREDIENTS:

Buffalo Quinoa Bites

½ cup quinoa

2½ cups water, divided

½ cup red lentils, picked through and rinsed

1 shallot, finely diced

3 cloves garlic, minced

3 tablespoons buffalo sauce

¼ teaspoon fine sea salt, or to taste

¼ teaspoon black pepper

1 teaspoon dried oregano

⅛ teaspoon ground cayenne (optional)

1 cup whole wheat bread crumbs (or 2 slices whole wheat bread, toasted and processed into crumbs)

1 large egg

1 tablespoon olive oil

INSTRUCTIONS:

1. Add the quinoa to a medium-sized pot and toast for a few minutes, stirring frequently. Add 1 cup of the water. Bring to a boil. Reduce heat to low, cover, and simmer for 15 to 20 minutes, until all the liquid is absorbed. Set aside to cool completely.

2. Combine the lentils with the remaining 1½ cups water in a medium-sized saucepan. Bring to a boil, then cover, reduce to a simmer, and cook for 10 minutes. The lentils will start to slightly break apart—that's okay. Thoroughly drain any excess water. Set aside to cool completely.

3. Combine the quinoa, lentils, shallot, garlic, buffalo sauce, salt, pepper, oregano, cayenne (if using), and bread crumbs. Stir to combine, and then stir in the egg.

4. Preheat the oven to 400°F.

5. Shape balls out of tablespoons of the mixture. The dough will still be sticky, so it will be easier to shape the balls with slightly wet hands. The recipe will make about 30 bites. Place on a parchment-lined baking sheet, and drizzle with olive oil. Bake 25 to 30 minutes, until lightly golden and set.

Feta Ranch

2   ounces feta cheese (goat cheese also works well)

1   cup 2% plain Greek yogurt

3   tablespoons light sour cream

1   tablespoon apple cider vinegar

⅛–¼ teaspoon fine sea salt

¼   teaspoon black pepper

1   teaspoon dried dill

½   tablespoon olive oil

6. While the quinoa bites are baking, combine all of the ranch ingredients in a food processor, and process until smooth.

7. Serve the warm bites with Feta Ranch dipping sauce.

NUTRITION INFORMATION PER SERVING:
Calories 145, Calories from Fat 49, Fat (g) 5.4, Saturated Fat (g) 2, Protein (g) 8.5, Carbohydrate (g) 15.8, Dietary Fiber (g) 3.3, Cholesterol (mg) 27, Sodium (mg) 311

CHAPTER SEVEN

SWEET SNACKS
AND DESSERTS

FUDGY PEANUT BUTTER SWIRL BROWNIES

SERVES 12

Rich, dark chocolate fudge brownies with a drizzle of peanut butter on top. These taste decadent, yet are made with no butter and less sugar than most brownie recipes, and are rich in fiber and protein because of the black beans hidden in the batter. Fool others with this healthy brownie recipe, or just keep them to yourself so you have a better-for-you treat on hand.

INGREDIENTS:

¼ cup unbleached all-purpose flour

½ cup unsweetened cocoa powder

⅛ teaspoon salt

1 (15-ounce) can black beans, drained and rinsed

½ cup 2% milk

½ cup granulated sugar

1 large egg

½ tablespoon vanilla extract

⅓ cup mini semisweet chocolate chips

½ cup creamy peanut butter, melted

INSTRUCTIONS:

1. Preheat the oven to 350°F.

2. Sift together the flour, cocoa powder, and salt. Set aside.

3. Combine the beans and milk in a food processor or blender, and process until mostly smooth (this will take a couple of minutes).

4. Transfer the milk and bean mixture to a mixing bowl. Beat in the sugar, then add the egg and vanilla and mix well.

5. Gradually mix the dry ingredients into the wet ingredients. Fold in the chocolate chips.

6. Pour half of the batter into an 8-inch square baking dish. Drizzle with half of the melted peanut butter. Top with the remaining batter and the remaining peanut butter.

7. Bake for 20 to 22 minutes, until a knife inserted in the center comes out clean. Allow to cool for 10 or 15 minutes, then slice into 12 bars.

8. These bars may be kept at room temperature, but I love how they taste when chilled in the fridge.

NUTRITION INFORMATION PER SERVING:
Calories 176, Calories from Fat 72, Fat (g) 8, Saturated Fat (g) 2.1, Protein (g) 6.5, Carbohydrate (g) 22.8, Dietary Fiber (g) 3.7, Cholesterol (mg) 22.8, Sodium (mg) 103

NO-BAKE CHERRY NUT ENERGY BITES

SERVES 4

When three o'clock rolls around and I have no snacks within reach, I start to freak out a bit. To avoid grabbing anything unhealthy (and unfilling) out of desperation, I like to keep healthy options at my desk. These bites are jam-packed with good-for-you ingredients like almonds, walnuts, and dried fruit. They taste rich and sweet, but have zero added sugar and are made up of just six simple ingredients. Whip these up on the weekend and you'll have a portable, protein-packed snack to get you through those between-meal hunger swings for the rest of the week.

INGREDIENTS:

- ½ cup slivered raw almonds
- ½ cup chopped raw walnuts
- ¼ cup dried, unsweetened dark cherries
- ¼ cup dried pitted dates (about 6 dates)
- ¼ teaspoon ground cinnamon
- 1 tablespoon natural almond butter with sea salt

INSTRUCTIONS:

1. Place all the ingredients in a food processor and pulse until very finely chopped. Test the mixture by grabbing some of it with your fingers and checking whether it sticks together. If it still crumbles a bit, keep processing.

2. Scoop out 2 tablespoons of the mixture, and use your hands to press together into a ball. Repeat with remaining mixture. The recipe will make eight balls in all.

NUTRITION INFORMATION PER SERVING:
Calories 276, Calories from Fat 177, Fat (g) 19.7, Saturated Fat (g) 1.8, Protein (g) 6.7, Carbohydrate (g) 22.4, Dietary Fiber (g) 4.8, Cholesterol (mg) 0, Sodium (mg) 12

LEMON RASPBERRY CHIA SEED MUFFINS

SERVES 12

I used to grab jumbo lemon poppy seed muffins from the cafeteria in college more often than I care to admit. The sweet-and-sour crunch of those muffins tasted refreshing, but the lack of protein and fiber would result in serious hunger pangs just an hour or two later. This version has less sugar than standard lemon poppy seed muffins, but it's full of that sweet-and-sour flavor from lemon zest, lemon juice, and fresh raspberries. Instead of poppy seeds, these muffins get their crunch from protein-packed chia seeds. To give the muffins a true bakery feel, I like to top them with sliced almonds and a bit of crunchy sparkling sugar.

INGREDIENTS:

½ cup granulated sugar

1 tablespoon lemon zest

2 cups whole wheat pastry flour

2 teaspoons baking powder

¼ teaspoon baking soda

¼ teaspoon salt

¼ cup fresh lemon juice

¾ cup plain nonfat Greek yogurt

2 large eggs

1 teaspoon vanilla extract

½ cup natural applesauce

3 tablespoons vegetable oil

¼ cup chia seeds

6 ounces fresh raspberries

½ cup sliced almonds, for topping

1 tablespoon sparkling sugar (optional), for topping

INSTRUCTIONS:

1. Preheat the oven to 400°F.

2. Rub together the sugar and lemon zest with your fingertips until fragrant. Whisk in the flour, baking powder, baking soda, and salt.

3. In a separate bowl, whisk together the lemon juice, yogurt, eggs, vanilla, applesauce, and oil.

4. Pour the wet ingredients over the dry ingredients and stir until just mixed. Fold in the chia seeds. Gently fold in the raspberries (you don't want them to break apart too much).

5. Divide the batter among 12 well-greased muffin tins (about one heaping quarter cup each). Top with sliced almonds, and sparkling sugar (if desired). The muffin tins will be very full—that's okay.

6. Bake for 20 to 25 minutes, until golden on top and a knife/toothpick inserted in the center comes out clean.

NUTRITION INFORMATION PER SERVING:
Calories 218, Calories from Fat 72, Fat (g) 8, Saturated Fat (g) 0.9, Protein (g) 6.3, Carbohydrate (g) 31.4, Dietary Fiber (g) 5.6, Cholesterol (mg) 31, Sodium (mg) 155

PEANUT BUTTER PROTEIN MUFFINS

SERVES 12

After looking through this book, you may have noticed I have a bit of an obsession with peanut butter. It's versatile, protein-packed, and I happen to believe it's one of the most perfect foods on this planet. These muffins are full of peanut butter flavor, plus tons of protein and fiber to keep you full for hours. They're great as is, but if you want a bit more sweetness, fold ⅓ cup of mini chocolate chips into the batter, or melt the chocolate chips and drizzle on top after baking.

INGREDIENTS:

- ¾ cup whole-grain spelt flour (or whole wheat pastry flour)
- ½ cup quick oats
- ¼ cup wheat germ
- 1 teaspoon baking powder
- ½ teaspoon baking soda
- ½ teaspoon ground cinnamon
- ¼ teaspoon salt
- ½ cup natural unsweetened applesauce
- ⅔ cup creamy peanut butter
- 3 tablespoons honey
- 3 tablespoons packed dark brown sugar
- 1 large egg
- 2 teaspoons vanilla extract
- ½ cup 2% plain Greek yogurt

INSTRUCTIONS:

1. Preheat the oven to 375°F.

2. Whisk together the flour, oats, wheat germ, baking powder, baking soda, cinnamon, and salt in a bowl. Set aside.

3. In another bowl, stir together the applesauce and peanut butter. Mix in the honey, sugar, egg, and vanilla, then whisk in the Greek yogurt.

4. Gradually mix the dry ingredients into the wet ingredients.

5. Drop the batter into 12 lined and greased muffin tins.

6. Bake for 15 to 18 minutes, until a toothpick or knife inserted in the center comes out clean.

7. Allow to cool completely. Store in an airtight container. Since this is an oil-free quick bread, the muffin flavor and texture will improve overnight.

NUTRITION INFORMATION PER SERVING:
Calories 184, Calories from Fat 76, Fat (g) 8.4, Saturated Fat (g) 1.2, Protein (g) 7, Carbohydrate (g) 21.4, Dietary Fiber (g) 2.8, Cholesterol (mg) 16, Sodium (mg) 197

ALMOND BUTTER BANANA FLAX MUFFINS WITH NUTELLA

SERVES 12

This is one of those recipes that walks the line between indulgent snack and healthier dessert. Three bananas, almond butter, and Greek yogurt keep these muffins super moist, without any oil or butter. Whole wheat pastry flour brings fiber and protein, yet its lighter texture keeps the dough from getting heavy. A tiny dab of chocolate-hazelnut spread in the center makes these muffins good enough to be dessert, even though you know in your heart that you're making a healthy choice.

INGREDIENTS:

1¼ cups whole wheat pastry flour

¼ cup ground flaxseed

¾ teaspoon baking powder

¼ teaspoon salt

3 medium-sized overripe bananas, mashed (about 1 cup)

½ cup natural creamy almond butter with sea salt

½ cup packed dark brown sugar

1 large egg

1½ teaspoons almond extract

½ cup 2% plain Greek yogurt

12 teaspoons chocolate-hazelnut spread (like Nutella)

INSTRUCTIONS:

1. Preheat the oven to 375°F.

2. Whisk together the flour, flaxseed, baking powder, and salt. Set aside.

3. Mix together the bananas and almond butter. Add the sugar, and beat until smooth. Mix in the egg and almond extract.

4. Slowly add the dry ingredients to the wet ingredients. Add the Greek yogurt and stir until fully incorporated, being careful not to overmix.

5. Line a muffin tin with liners and coat them with nonstick spray. Scoop a heaping tablespoon of batter into each liner. Drop in 1 teaspoon chocolate-hazelnut spread. Top with another heaping tablespoon of batter.

6. Bake for 20 to 22 minutes, until lightly golden on top, and a toothpick inserted in the center comes out clean.

NUTRITION INFORMATION PER SERVING:
Calories 234, Calories from Fat 87, Fat (g) 9.7, Saturated Fat (g) 1.8, Protein (g) 6.1, Carbohydrate (g) 32.5, Dietary Fiber (g) 4.4, Cholesterol (mg) 16, Sodium (mg) 111

CREAMY LIME PIE

SERVES 12

Ryan ate this pie for lunch the day I made it, and as he was eating he asked why an empty tofu container sat on the counter. "I haven't had time to clean up yet," I explained. He responded with, "Wasn't that from the stir-fry yesterday?" I laughed and told him that no, I was referring to the pie he was currently devouring. "This? This pie is made with tofu? What part? How? . . ." His questioning and confusion continued as he finished every last bite. This pie is so creamy, flavorful, and smooth that no one, not even my carnivorous counterpart, would ever suspect (or care) that it's entirely vegan and made with protein-rich tofu.

INGREDIENTS:

Almond Crust

2   cups almond meal

1   cup whole wheat pastry flour

1½ tablespoons cane sugar

½   teaspoon ground cinnamon

⅛   teaspoon fine sea salt

¼   cup coconut oil, melted

2   tablespoons water

Creamy Lime Filling

14   ounces organic soft tofu

½   cup fresh lime juice

1¼ cups cane sugar

2   tablespoons lime zest

3   tablespoons unbleached all-purpose flour

3   tablespoons cornstarch

Coconut Whipped Cream (optional)

1   cup coconut cream, refrigerated overnight

⅛   teaspoon vanilla extract

1–2 tablespoons powdered sugar

INSTRUCTIONS:

1. Preheat the oven to 350°F.

2. Place all the dry crust ingredients in a bowl and use a fork to combine. Pour in the oil and water, and stir until the dough is fully moistened.

3. Transfer the crust to a liberally greased 9-inch pie or round cake pan. Use your fingers to firmly press the crust into the bottom and up the sides of the pan. You want to pack it in tight so that it does not crumble. Poke holes in the surface of the crust with a fork.

4. Bake the crust for 20 to 25 minutes, until lightly golden.

5. Place the tofu in a food processor and process until it turns into fine crumbs. Add the lime juice and sugar and blend until completely smooth (test to ensure that all of the sugar has been blended). Add the lime zest, flour, and cornstarch, and pulse until combined.

6. Pour the filling into the pan. Tap it on the counter a few times to release any air bubbles.

7. Place the pan in the oven and bake for 25 to 30 minutes, until the sides are set but the middle is still a bit jiggly. Let cool completely, and then place in the refrigerator to chill for at least 1 hour.

**NUTRITION INFORMATION PER SERVING
(1 SLICE OF PIE):**

Calories 318, Calories from Fat 141, Fat (g) 15.6,
Saturated Fat (g) 4.7, Protein (g) 7.5,
Carbohydrate (g) 38.6, Dietary Fiber (g) 3.6,
Cholesterol (mg) 0, Sodium (mg) 29

**NUTRITION INFORMATION PER SERVING
(1⁄12 OF COCONUT CREAM):**

Calories 47, Calories from Fat 36, Fat (g) 4,
Saturated Fat (g) 3.8, Protein (g) 0.5,
Carbohydrate (g) 2, Dietary Fiber (g) 0,
Cholesterol (mg) 0, Sodium (mg) 6

You can serve the pie at room temperature, but it will be much more difficult to cut, so it is best to let it chill.

8. If you're serving with coconut whipped cream, place a large metal bowl and beater in the refrigerator for 10 to 15 minutes. Place the cream in the chilled bowl and beat on high until whipped. Add the vanilla and sugar and whip again into soft peaks.

9. When you're ready to serve, spoon coconut whipped cream (or dairy whipped cream) onto the chilled pie before slicing, or dollop cream onto individual pieces.

CHOCOLATE CUPCAKES WITH PEANUT BUTTER VANILLA BEAN FROSTING

SERVES 18

Since I need at least one sweet bite every day, I'm always trying to find ways to lighten up my favorite treats. These cupcakes have a rich dark chocolate flavor, and an unbelievably moist and fluffy texture, yet are made without butter or eggs. Instead of a rich and decadent buttercream, I frosted these cupcakes with a creamy Greek yogurt peanut butter vanilla bean frosting. If you want to add some variety, swap the peanut butter in the frosting with Nutella for an extra chocolaty treat.

INGREDIENTS:

Chocolate Cupcakes

½   cup 1% low-fat milk

½   tablespoon apple cider vinegar

1   (16-ounce) container silken tofu

3   tablespoons coconut oil, melted

¾   cup packed dark brown sugar

½   tablespoon vanilla extract

1¼ cups unbleached all-purpose flour

½   cup whole wheat pastry flour

¾   cup cocoa powder

½   tablespoon baking soda

¼   teaspoon salt

½   cup strong coffee

Peanut Butter Greek Yogurt Frosting

1¼ cups 2% plain Greek yogurt

½   cup peanut butter

2   tablespoons mascarpone cheese

¾   cup powdered sugar

Seeds from 1 vanilla bean

INSTRUCTIONS:

1. Preheat the oven to 350°F.

2. Combine the milk and apple cider vinegar, and set aside for 5 minutes.

3. Puree the tofu in a food processor until completely smooth. Transfer to a large mixing bowl, then beat in the coconut oil and brown sugar. Beat in the vanilla and milk-vinegar mixture until smooth.

4. In a separate bowl, sift together the flours, cocoa powder, baking soda, and salt.

5. Gradually add the dry ingredients to the wet ingredients.

6. Pour in the hot coffee and stir until it is distributed throughout the batter.

7. Place muffin liners in a muffin pan, and liberally grease with nonstick spray. Scoop the batter into the muffin liners using a quarter cup. You should end up with 18 cupcakes.

8. Bake for 15 to 20 minutes, or until a knife inserted in the center comes out clean.

9. Place on a cooling rack to cool completely.

10. For the frosting, whip together the Greek yogurt, peanut butter, and mascarpone. Beat in the sugar and vanilla seeds.

11. Use a spoon to dollop frosting on top of each cooled cupcake.

NUTRITION INFORMATION PER SERVING:
Calories 205, Calories from Fat 74, Fat (g) 8.3, Saturated Fat (g) 3.5, Protein (g) 6.8, Carbohydrate (g) 28.4, Dietary Fiber (g) 2.3, Cholesterol (mg) 4, Sodium (mg) 184

ALMOND, CHERRY, AND QUINOA GRANOLA

SERVES 14

Homemade granola is not only tastier than the store-bought variety, but also more affordable, and you can customize it to your tastes. Quinoa and chia seeds add extra crunch to the oat and almond butter clusters in this version, while honey and brown sugar lightly sweeten each bite. Feel free to swap in different nuts and dried fruits, or even add some chocolate chips for a little extra sweetness.

INGREDIENTS:

1   cup quinoa, uncooked

2   cups old-fashioned rolled oats

2   tablespoons chia seeds

¼   cup packed brown sugar

¼   teaspoon salt

½   cup slivered raw almonds

¼   cup hulled raw pepitas

½   cup unsweetened flaked coconut

2   tablespoons coconut oil, measured solid

½   cup natural salted almond butter

¼   cup natural applesauce

3   tablespoons honey

½   teaspoon almond extract

½   cup dried cherries

INSTRUCTIONS:

1. Preheat the oven to 300°F.

2. Mix together the quinoa, oats, chia seeds, brown sugar, salt, almonds, pepitas, and coconut in a large bowl.

3. In a microwave-safe bowl or in a small saucepan over medium heat, melt the coconut oil and almond butter together. Remove from the heat and stir in the applesauce, honey, and almond extract.

4. Pour the wet ingredients into the dry ingredients, and stir until the mixture is evenly coated.

5. Transfer to a parchment-lined baking sheet, and bake for 30 to 40 minutes, stirring frequently, until golden brown.

6. Allow to cool completely, then stir in the dried cherries.

NUTRITION INFORMATION PER SERVING:
Calories 277, Calories from Fat 126, Fat (g) 14, Saturated Fat (g) 4.6, Protein (g) 7.2, Carbohydrate (g) 33, Dietary Fiber (g) 4.9, Cholesterol (mg) 0, Sodium (mg) 67

Note: If you're eating this granola for breakfast, serving it with ½ cup 1 percent cow's milk adds 4.1 g protein; ½ cup plain soy milk adds 3.5 g protein.

PEANUT BUTTER CHOCOLATE CHIP GRANOLA BARS

SERVES 12

I'm a big fan of swirling peanut butter into my oatmeal to give it a little extra protein and flavor. With these granola bars, I can enjoy those same flavors (plus chocolate) in a hearty, filling snack. They're filled with tons of nutritious, protein-rich ingredients, yet they're also sweet enough to be kid-friendly. If you want a chocolate-free snack, you can simply omit the chips, or stir your favorite dried fruit into the oat mixture instead.

INGREDIENTS:

1¾ cups old-fashioned oats

¼ cup whole wheat pastry flour

3 tablespoons ground flaxseed

¼ teaspoon salt

½ teaspoon ground cinnamon

¼ cup roasted salted peanuts, chopped

2 tablespoons coconut oil

½ cup creamy peanut butter

3 tablespoons lightly packed dark brown sugar

3 tablespoons honey

½ tablespoon vanilla extract

1 egg white

2 tablespoons mini semisweet chocolate chips

INSTRUCTIONS:

1. Preheat the oven to 350°F.

2. Combine the oats, flour, flaxseed, salt, cinnamon, and peanuts in a bowl.

3. In a microwave-safe container, melt the coconut oil and peanut butter together (this took about 20 seconds in my microwave). Once melted, stir in the sugar, honey, and vanilla. Pour the wet mixture into the oat mixture, and stir until the dry ingredients are coated.

4. Touch the mixture to make sure it isn't hot; if it is hot, let it cool for a few minutes. Mix in the egg white, stirring until evenly distributed.

5. Coat an 8 x 8-inch baking dish with nonstick spray. Line with parchment, and pour in the oat mixture. Using another piece of parchment paper or plastic wrap, press the mixture firmly into the dish. Sprinkle with chocolate chips, and press them lightly into the oats.

6. Bake for 25 to 30 minutes until golden on the edges. Allow to cool before cutting into 12 bars.

NUTRITION INFORMATION PER SERVING:
Calories 205, Calories from Fat 104, Fat (g) 11.5, Saturated Fat (g) 3.5, Protein (g) 6, Carbohydrate (g) 21.3, Dietary Fiber (g) 3, Cholesterol (mg) 0, Sodium (mg) 123

CRUNCHY VANILLA BROWN SUGAR ALMOND BUTTER

SERVES 14

All my life I've been obsessed with peanut butter, but it wasn't until five years ago that I discovered my love for almond butter. It tastes so rich, smooth, and decadent that it's hard to believe it's actually a healthy snack. This version is lightly sweetened with dark brown sugar and vanilla extract, which are balanced out by a touch of sea salt. I added golden flaxseeds for crunch, but feel free to leave them out if you wish. I tend to eat almond butter straight from the jar, but it also goes great on toast, graham crackers, fruit, or in any recipe in this book that calls for natural almond butter.

INGREDIENTS:

3 cups unsalted roasted almonds

2 teaspoons vanilla extract

1½ tablespoons lightly packed dark brown sugar

¼ teaspoon fine sea salt

2 tablespoons golden flaxseeds (optional)

INSTRUCTIONS:

1. Place the almonds in a large food processor or high-powered blender. Process on low for 5 minutes, then boost up to high. Process until smooth—this may take anywhere from 15 to 30 minutes, depending on your food processor's size and power.

2. Once the almonds reach the consistency you like, add the vanilla, sugar, and salt, and pulse a few times to combine. Taste and adjust the sugar and salt levels to your liking.

3. Remove the blade from the processor, pour in the flaxseeds, and use a spoon to stir.

4. Store in an airtight container in the refrigerator.

NUTRITION INFORMATION PER SERVING:
Calories 189, Calories from Fat 142, Fat (g) 15.8, Saturated Fat (g) 1.2, Protein (g) 6.4, Carbohydrate (g) 8.1, Dietary Fiber (g) 3.5, Cholesterol (mg) 0, Sodium (mg) 44

The High-Protein Vegetarian Cookbook

RICOTTA AND MASCARPONE BAKED APPLES WITH SALTED CARAMEL

SERVES 4

These apples are like a big autumnal hug. The ricotta-mascarpone filling is creamy and perfectly sweetened; the notes of cinnamon and dark brown sugar make it feel incredibly warm and comforting. The different layers of flavor—the tart apple, the creamy cheese, and the salted caramel—make for a seemingly complex (but secretly simple), decadent treat.

INGREDIENTS:

Baked Apples

4 large Honeycrisp apples

1 cup part-skim ricotta

3 tablespoons mascarpone cheese

¼ teaspoon ground cinnamon

2 tablespoons lightly packed dark brown sugar

1 tablespoon butter

¾ cup boiling water

Salted Caramel

¼ cup packed dark brown sugar

1½ tablespoons water

2 tablespoons unsalted butter, cut into chunks

3 tablespoons half-and-half

1 teaspoon vanilla extract

⅛ teaspoon sea salt (or other coarse salt)

NUTRITION INFORMATION PER SERVING:
Calories 422, Calories from Fat 180, Fat (g) 20.1, Saturated Fat (g) 12.4, Protein (g) 8.8, Carbohydrate (g) 55.7, Dietary Fiber (g) 5.4, Cholesterol (mg) 63, Sodium (mg) 173

INSTRUCTIONS:

1. Preheat the oven to 375°F.

2. Use a paring knife to core the apples. I cut at a slight angle, and then used a spoon to scoop out the core of the apple. Make sure you get rid of all the seeds.

3. Place the cored apples in an 8- or 9-inch baking dish.

4. Place the ricotta, mascarpone, cinnamon, and brown sugar in a food processor or blender. Process until smooth.

5. Divide the cheese filling among the four apples. Top each with ¼ tablespoon butter.

6. Pour the boiling water into the dish with the apples. Bake for 30 to 40 minutes, until you can easily cut through the apples with a fork, but they aren't overly mushy.

7. While the apples bake, get the caramel together: Over medium heat, combine the brown sugar and water. When it starts to boil, add the butter and whisk until it starts to boil again. Add the half-and-half and vanilla, and boil for 3 to 5 minutes, whisking constantly. Remove from heat and stir in the salt.

8. After removing the apples from the oven, use a spoon to pour the pan juices over them.

9. Drizzle each baked apple with caramel sauce. Serve with vanilla ice cream, if desired.

ACKNOWLEDGMENTS

KATIE

It's impossible for me to thank the many people who helped make this book happen on this one page, but to all those who tasted, critiqued, and supported me through this whirlwind experience - THANK YOU!

A big thanks and hug to Ryan, for living with this messy cook, and being open to trying (and liking!) bean brownies and tofu pie.

Thank you to my amazing family, and particularly my sister Anna, for taking so many leftovers off my hands.

Special thanks to my awesome co-author Kristen for combing through all of the recipes with her knowledgeable nutritionist eye.

And finally to Ann, my publisher, for reaching out with the book idea in the first place, and making a dream of mine become a reality.

ACKNOWLEDGMENTS

KRISTEN

To my wonderful family and friends, thank you for your excitement, valuable feedback and encouragement throughout this entire process.

A huge thank you full of love and appreciation goes to my husband and daughter for being my biggest supporters.

To the excellent folks at WW Norton, thank you for your guidance and expertise in taking this cookbook from concept to completion.

And finally to Katie, the genius behind these wonderful recipes, thank you for asking me to be a part of such a delicious project!

INDEX

The High-Protein Vegetarian Cookbook

The High-Protein Vegetarian Cookbook

The High-Protein Vegetarian Cookbook